Presented To:

~

____

From:

~

____

Date:

~

____

Isaiah 61: Your Mission

Should You Choose to Accept It

Isaiah 61: Your Mission

Should You Choose to Accept It

A 30-Day Devotional Journey By

Brad Fenichel

Author of *Curse of the Skunk People*

Originally Serialized on the National Minute of Prayer Blog

Jordan Strikers Press™
Elkton, Maryland 21921

ISAIAH 61: YOUR MISSION (Should You Choose to Accept It)
Published by Jordan Strikers Press™, an imprint of Saddle Mountain Communications™, Elkton, Maryland 21921

ISBN-13: 978-1-955510-02-8
Library of Congress Control Number: 2023919397

Printed in the United States of America
2023 — First Edition

10 9 8 7 6 5 4 3 2 1

I dedicate this book to all "Blessed Mourners."

May the one true Comforter, the Holy Spirit Who was present with our Lord Jesus Christ as He inaugurated His earthly ministry, fill your own cup to overflowing with passion and boldness for the Mission.

- Brad Fenichel

"... The LORD has anointed Me ... to console those who mourn in Zion ... And they shall rebuild ... raise up ... and repair ..."

(Isaiah 61:1b-4, NKJV)

Contents

Preface ix
Also from Brad Fenichel xiii
1. Passing the Mantle 15
2. You Can't Fit a Square Foot into a Round Slipper 21
3. Mr. Bell's Fixit Shop 25
4. Tertiary Adjunct of Unimatrix Zero-One 29
5. Aloft in a Body Bag 33
6. Peace, Beaver! 37
7. Truman's Beard and The Clock Strikes Twelve 41
8. Palmer's Disease? I'm Good with That! 45
9. Smokey Bear Says, 'Let It Burn!' 49
10. Joe Cool and the Gold Rush Girls 55
11. Horsie Rides with Haman 61
12. Plant My Head on the Front Seat 67
13. Lushness of Hell 75
14. How to Make the Cover of *Forbes* 79
15. How to Refit Your Cellar for Use as a Septic Tank 83
16. And Ye Shall Be Named ... 'Foreign Devil'? 89
17. Dost Covet Destruction, Thou Maniac? 95
18. 'Soupe au Caillou': Miracle Recipe from the Bible 103
19. Waiting for Normal Body Parts to Arrive 107
20. Cracking Nuts in Jesus' Name 113
21. Jesus: Life of the Party? 119
22. She Needs Shoes! 125
23. Robbery for Burnt Offering 129
24. Uncover before Narnia, You Dog! 133
25. One if by Bondage, Two if by Blood 139
26. Seeds That Bless, Seeds That Crush 145
27. Nerves Aflame 153
28. Queen of Diamonds, King of Hearts 159
29. Jesus' Views on Bud-Light 163
30. Megatonnage! 167
About the Author 175

PREFACE

> So He came to Nazareth, where He had been brought up. And as His custom was, He went into the synagogue on the Sabbath day, and stood up to read. And He was handed the book of the prophet Isaiah. And when He had opened the book, He found the place where it was written:
>
> "The Spirit of the Lord is upon Me, because He has anointed Me to preach the gospel to the poor; He has sent Me to heal the brokenhearted, to proclaim liberty to the captives and recovery of sight to the blind, to set at liberty those who are oppressed; to proclaim the acceptable year of the Lord."
>
> Then He closed the book, and gave it back to the attendant and sat down. And the eyes of all who were in the synagogue were fixed on Him. And He began to say to them, "Today this Scripture is fulfilled in your hearing." (Luke 4:16-21, NKJV)

Isaiah—considered by many to be the greatest of all prophets used to pen our Lord's holy Scriptures. The only one who was called, ordained, and commissioned in the very throne room of Almighty God. Doubtless, the people of Nazareth were brimming with pride that their own little synagogue possessed a scroll containing the complete Book of Isaiah.

And of all the resplendent, transcendent passages contained in Isaiah's magnificent scroll, Jesus chose on that Sabbath day to quote from chapter 61 for His great inaugural address. Yet, the interesting part is not merely what He read from the chapter, but where He stopped reading! For, of the eleven verses (as we parse it today) that comprise Isaiah 61, He ready only the first verse, followed by half of the second ... and, in fact, broke off mid-sentence. After which, He rolled it back up, handed it to the scroll-keeper, and returned to His seat.

Of course, the punch line wasn't long in coming. When the crowd pinned Him down with their gaze, as if to say, "Is that all!?" He quietly let drop the last shoe: "Oh, yeah. You know, of course, that Isaiah wrote that about *Me*. About *today*." Which, of course, did not go over well at all!

But *why* did Jesus seemingly cut His reading short? We know He could well have preached three chapters' worth of material, as He did quite soon thereafter at the Sermon on the Mount. So, at least He could have read this entire Isaiah portion down to where it ended.

This book attempts to unpack the mysteries of Isaiah 61, *including* why Jesus unsealed just that verse-and-a-half to launch His earthly ministry. And why the balance of the chapter was a bequest reserved for His disciples, starting with the twelve and continuing right down to—and through—you and me! We'll explore the "Year of the Lord" and His "Day of Vengeance." We'll discover the "Blessed Mourners" for whom Christ has unsealed Isaiah's full sixty-first chapter as His "Messianic Playbook," infused with the purpose and power by which they are to go forth and turn their upside-down world right side up.

"Without Me you can do nothing," Christ told them at the Last Supper. We need Jesus more than the air we breathe, and we need His Word just as the natural bread that keeps our bodies alive. But if we read that Word offhandedly, never delving into the *why* of His purposes and commissions for our tenure on this planet, then we miss the whole point and run the risk of becoming spiritual "castaways"—as the Apostle Paul put it. Of wasting our God-given potential.

It's like the man who won the lottery, bought himself a brand-new private airplane, and then ... never took flying lessons. He just taxied the thing out onto the freeway, intending to "drive" it to visit a friend in the next state. Of course, he ended up abandoning the plane alongside the road after the engine overheated and seized up! Why? Because this piece of equipment was not built for earthly travel. It was designed to go up! Likewise, you and I were designed to go up. And Isaiah 61 reveals, in step-by-step detail, our Lord's purpose, design, and provision for us to go up.

Isaiah 61 has always had a powerful drawn on my spirit. It started when I was just twelve. This was during the peak years of the Jesus People movement, when my father, who was a pastor and missionary, felt a calling to establish a training center for the many young people getting saved through "coffee house" ministries, and who felt a desire to be used of God on the mission field.

Sadly, over many years, the training center fell short of its mission and the constituents ultimately disbanded, partly—as so often happens with those of us whom God calls—as a consequence of my father's Samson-like blind spots and vulnerabilities. But that's a topic I plan to explore further in my upcoming book, *The Fall of Sion.*

Back to when I was twelve years old. The ministry purchased a 1950s Studebaker school bus, for something like $100, from a junkyard owner who said it had been retired because of a "catastrophic water leak coming from the engine." As it turns out, about $20 worth of freeze plugs was all it took to get *Lazarus*—as we christened the bus—back from the dead and onto the highway.

So, about 20 passionate young Jesus freaks packed into *Lazarus* for a mission adventure. We were to travel two states away, with the goal of preaching to the thousands of devotees of Guru Maharaj Ji—a 15-year-old proclaimed by his followers as a "reincarnation of Jesus Christ"—who had rented the Houston Astrodome to host a mega-convention.

Each morning of this two-week mission trip began with a 30-minute devotional time where we would read out loud the entire chapter of Isaiah 61, followed by open conversation about how it might apply to us. It was great idea—we all admired the divine gift of such a flowery Bible passage and commented on its inspirational effects. Yet we never went as far as to unpack this Messianic Playbook verse by verse—to read the instructions on how to "fly" it as the Holy Spirit intended. And at the end of the two-week jaunt, we simply shelved the chapter and never studied it again.

In retrospect, I see this as a profound tragedy. The Fall of Sion could have been avoided, and the Kingdom purposes of God fulfilled back in our day, if we had simply paid attention. If we had unpacked and assimilated this glorious chapter, this aircraft manual that could lift our Kingdom vision and impact from the earthly level to the heavenlies. Of course, we weren't the only Christians down through the ages who failed to grasp what was right before us. But Isaiah 61 is still in the Bible, right where our Lord put it. It's time to "break the glass" and use what He's given us "for such a time as this."

It is my fervent prayer that this book will afford a 30-day window of opportunity, in time and eternity, for you and me to pause and *let sink in* the glorious wealth of promise packed into the eleven verses of Isaiah 61. Let us answer the call to become one of His Blessed Mourners, instructed and empowered to go forth and be His hand extended, to be salt of the earth and light of the world.

And finally, a word on this book's structure and style. Being of the devotional genre, it is served out in thirty chapters to inspire a month of daily prayer and meditation. Furthermore, the reader will notice a conversational, "fireside chat" tone, usually centered on an anecdote or popular quotation, but quite often alluding to current dates and events when it was written. That is because these thirty devotional segments were originally serialized over a thirty-month period on the National Minute of Prayer blog site, www.Facebook.com/MinuteOfPrayer.org. And, rather than sanitize the material of all its "bloggishness," I have elected to present it in its original form and character.

While reading these devotionals, meditating on the timeless message of Isaiah 61, and praying the prayer at the end of each chapter, may you see—with the eyes of your spirit—our Lord Christ Himself standing as He did before Thomas (in John 20), inviting you to touch His hands and His side, and then to go forth in the faith and power of that life-changing touch, to turn your world right side up for Him!

—Brad Fenichel, 2023
Founder, National Minute of Prayer
Author of *Curse of the Skunk People*

ALSO FROM BRAD FENICHEL

The Big Ben Minute – By Andrew Dakers

"IN UNITY IS STRENGTH"
Reaching across the threshold of a century, historian Andrew Herbert Dakers proffers the one "secret weapon"—concerted prayer—that can guarantee victory over the forces of moral and spiritual decay that even now threaten to destroy our Free World from within. Originally published in 1943, it is the most comprehensive narrative of the Big Ben Minute of prayer that contributed to Britain's courage and ultimate triumph against the Third Reich.

The Big Ben Minute (2012 Edition) includes a preface by Brad Fenichel, founder of the National Minute of Prayer, and a new foreword by the author's grandsons, Alan and Stewart Dakers, who granted permission for Saddle Mountain Communications and Brad Fenichel to bring this book back to print.

***The Big Ben Minute* is available at Amazon.com.**

Curse of the Skunk People – By Brad Fenichel

"A DAUNTLESS QUEST FOR SUBSTANCE IN A WORLD OF MAKE-BELIEVE"
Willi Wagner, a young Anabaptist, fled his native Germany in 1916 on a pilgrimage that would take him deep into the forgotten sierras of Central Mexico in his search for the legendary Skunk People. At stake ... the very notion that God still cares to be involved with men and women in our own time.

Wagner's dogged tenacity, through triumph and tragedy, stands as an inspiration for those of us who would dare—as he did—to believe that God not only exists, but also rewards those who diligently seek Him.

Told in parable form, the story is a challenge for each of us to break through the walls in our prayer closet—to connect with a God Who listens, and Who answers—to experience personal revival and fulfillment of His purposes for us in our generation.

WARNING: You will NOT be able to put this book down!

A bonus 40-page Study Guide is included for personal devotion and small group dialogue.

***Curse of the Skunk People* is available at Amazon.com**

1
Passing the Mantle

"The Spirit of the Lord God is upon Me, because the Lord has anointed [and] commissioned Me to ..." (Isaiah 61:1a, AMP)

"Supreme Court Justice Ruth Bader Ginsburg Dies at 87," read the NPR headline of September 18, 2020. Now, all political opinions aside—*and I mean that!*—most adults living in the U.S.A. and reading that headline knew, not only who it was referring to, but the gravity of the news.

You see, focusing on Ruth Bader Ginsburg *as a person* ... She had not only worn **the robe** of a United States Supreme Court justice; she had "been **the robe**." Regardless whether one agreed or disagreed with her legal (or personal) opinions, there was no denying that Justice Ginsburg's sincerity and demeanor—whether on or off the bench—bordered on nobility. And **the robe** she wore, though it was by far tinier than the other eight justices' robes, would be difficult to fill indeed.

This is the first installment in a series of devotionals based on Isaiah 61—the passage quoted by Jesus (in Luke 4) as He began His public ministry.

Now, this verse isn't just about Jesus bursting on the scene flashing his "badge" of authority—though that's precisely what He was doing—but it goes way further, foreshadowing the commission He was going to pass on to the Church (i.e., His disciples and their disciples, and ultimately, **yes**! ... you and me) within a few short years.

#1 "The Spirit of the Lord God is upon Me ..."

Wait! If Jesus was (and is) God, then how or why should the Spirit of God—the Holy Spirit—rest upon Him? There isn't room enough here to list the vast number of references in Scripture that allude to the Spirit of God resting on Jesus. But, just focusing on the context of Luke 4 (when Jesus quoted this passage), we see the progression:

a) Jesus is baptized by John (Luke 3:21)
b) The Holy Spirit descends upon Him as a dove (verse 22)
c) This marks the beginning of His ministry (verse 23)
d) Jesus was "filled with" and "led by" the Spirit (chapter 4:1)
e) He "returned [from the wilderness] in the power of the Spirit" (verse 14)
f) And finally, he stood up and read this very passage: "The Spirit of the Lord God is upon Me ..." (verses 16-19)

#2 "... **Because** the Lord has anointed [and] commissioned Me **to** ...

So, **because** Jesus was the Christ—the Messiah, the Anointed One—and **because** that anointing was a commission **to**—for the purpose of—accomplishing the things He was sent to do (which we'll examine in later devotionals) ... therefore, the Holy Spirit had to come upon Him and abide (remain) upon Him throughout His earthly ministry.

Now, it's clear that Jesus' ministry was all carried out, from that point forward, in the anointing and power of the Spirit. The same Spirit who descended in appearance as a dove and rested upon Him.

Since the days of the Levitical priesthood, God had ordained that anointing should be accompanied by physical symbolism, which was usually oil (from which we get the very word "anointing").

Sometimes the symbolism was different. God told Elijah to go "anoint Elisha son of Shaphat from Abel Meholah to succeed you as prophet." (1 Kings 19:16) But instead of pouring oil on Elisha's head, Elijah threw his own robe (mantle) over Elisha, and that had the same effect—a physical depiction of the Spirit Who would rest upon Elisha, giving him both the power and the authority to carry out his prophetic commission. And when Elijah was caught up to heaven (2 Kings 2), his robe descended upon Elisha, who immediately used it to perform the miracle that began his ministry—parting the Jordan.

Now, back to Justice Ruth Bader Ginsburg. She had worn the robe for twenty-seven years—a robe that symbolized her authority as one of nine persons representing the highest circle of justice in the United States of America. But the time had now come for another to wear that robe.

In the realm of the Spirit, just as Elijah's robe (mantle) passed to Elisha, there can be a passing of the anointing to a new vessel. Besides Elijah's case, we see Moses passing the anointing to Joshua, Aaron to Eleazar, and many other examples, though they did not all involve the same precise ritual or symbolism.

So, what does this have to do with you and me? Everything, really!

If our only purpose were to get into Heaven, why, we would all be caught up like Elijah the moment we became believers, would we not? But Elijah had already been serving the purposes of God for many years before he was finally taken. And, when the robe of anointing passed to Elisha, he also continued that God-ordained work for many more years, until death took him. In other words, as long as we're on this planet, it's because there is something for us to do.

Let's look once more at Jesus' reading of Isaiah 61:1. "The Spirit of the Lord God is upon Me, because the Lord has anointed [and] commissioned Me to ..." Now, once again, we'll devote later devotionals to delving deeper into the many infinitives that follow on that ponderous word "**to**."

But, suffice it to say that Jesus came to Earth to accomplish, by His Holy Spirit power and anointing, a God-size work of ministry ... not to mention His ultimate work of becoming the Sacrifice Lamb to atone for all Sin! And, accomplish it He did! But then He left, and ... *was that it?* Indeed no, hallelujah!

When Jesus spoke with His disciples after his resurrection and before His ascension, that's where he passed the robe—the anointing—for them to carry on that very same ministry: "So Jesus said to them again, 'Peace to you! As the Father has sent Me, I also send you.' And when He had said this, He breathed on them, and said to them, Receive the Holy Spirit.'" (John 20:21-22)

From that moment forth, "the Spirit of the Lord God" was upon his disciples because the Lord Jesus had "anointed [and] commissioned" them. He had SENT them to continue the same ministry that the Father had **sent** Him to begin.

Of course, it was formalized about seven weeks later on the Day of Pentecost, when the Holy Spirit anointing fell, not only upon them, but on 120 disciples gathered in the upper room—representing the first sprouts of the Early Church. And to this day, the Holy Spirit is given freely by God "to those who obey Him" (Acts 5:32), giving us, the Church, not only the robe of authority, but also the power to effectively continue the ministry of Jesus Christ (Acts 1:8).

Justice Ginsburg was an inspiration to all Americans—whether they agreed or disagreed with her—because she wore her tiny robe with such towering dignity until the very day she had to pass it to another.

Why not pray ...

"Dear Father, open my eyes to discover my own robe of anointing. May I take the first step today, reaching outside myself to continue the ministry of Jesus Christ. In the words of the old hymn, let me 'Be His hand extended / Reaching out to the oppressed / Let me touch Him—let me touch Jesus / So that others may know and be blessed.'
In Jesus' name. Amen"

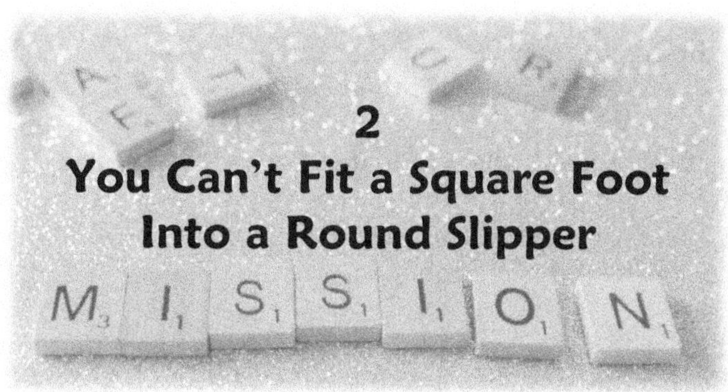

2
You Can't Fit a Square Foot Into a Round Slipper

"...The Lord has anointed [and] commissioned Me to bring good news to the humble and afflicted..." (Isaiah 61:1b, AMP)

> There, on a hazel tree, sat two pigeons, crying out:
> *Rook di goo, rook di goo!*
> *There's blood in the shoe.*
> *The shoe is too tight.*
> *This bride is not right!*

Just another sweet little G-rated fairy tale by that 19th-century duo, The Brothers Grimm. When I was six years old, my mother would read me a fairy tale every bedtime. But purist that she was, they had to be from the same dusty old tomes of Hans Christian Andersen and The Brothers Grimm that she had cut her own teeth on a few decades earlier.

Funny thing ... I never experienced childhood trauma or suffered nightmares with scenes of bloody mayhem such as Cinderella's prissy siblings dismembering their own feet—one removing her toes, and the other, her heel—to fit into the golden shoe. (And no, it was **not** a glass slipper! That was a Disney thing.)

Continuing the story ... once the hazel-pigeons had ratted out those two little angels with their reengineered feet ...

"Don't you have another daughter?" asked the prince.

"No," said the father. "Only a deformed little Cinderella from my first wife, but she cannot possibly be the bride."

"No indeed," agreed the stepmother, "She is much too dirty. She cannot be seen."

But the prince insisted on it, and ... you know the rest of the story.

"The Lord has anointed Me to bring good news to the poor," our Savior said, reading in the synagogue from Isaiah 61. (Or "the meek." Or "the humble and afflicted," as rendered by other translations.)

It's interesting to note that the Cinderella story has been retold in various forms and by numerous cultures since—by curious coincidence—right about the time of Jesus' own life and ministry on Earth. Fairy tales, as a genre, have been common currency across the ages because they contain the stuff of life: the wealthy and the poor, the lofty and the afflicted, good vs. evil, hope vs. despair.

This world's wise and wealthy expect divine favor by virtue of their status. Sure, I'll squeeze my foot into the Prince's golden slipper. What's a extra few toes, between friends? But Jesus didn't come to rub elbows with the wise and wealthy (unless they set those things aside to follow Him, of course); He came to bring good news to regular people like you and me. Because those lofty folk had "blood in the shoe."

In the Parable of the Great Banquet, after all the influential guests scorned the Lord's invitation, he "... became angry and ordered his servant, 'Go out quickly into the streets and alleys of the town and bring in the poor, the crippled, the blind and the lame.'" (Luke 14:21, NIV)

The Wise Men sought Jesus in a king's palace ... but the shepherds had already found him lying in a manger. The chief priests and rulers expected a Messiah in shining armor, riding forth to crush the Roman occupation ... but the "humble and afflicted" had already found a lowly Carpenter riding a donkey into Jerusalem where He would make the ultimate sacrifice and break their yoke of affliction.

What does this mean for us, His disciples? "As the Father has sent Me, so also I am sending you," said Jesus before ascending to his throne.

Why not pray ...

"Dear Father, forgive me for all the ways I've favored people for their status, their wealth, and all the other things this world values, and ignored the poor, the humble, and the afflicted. Fill me with the love of Jesus so I'll be a bearer of good news to the poor and afflicted who cross my path.
In Jesus' name. Amen"

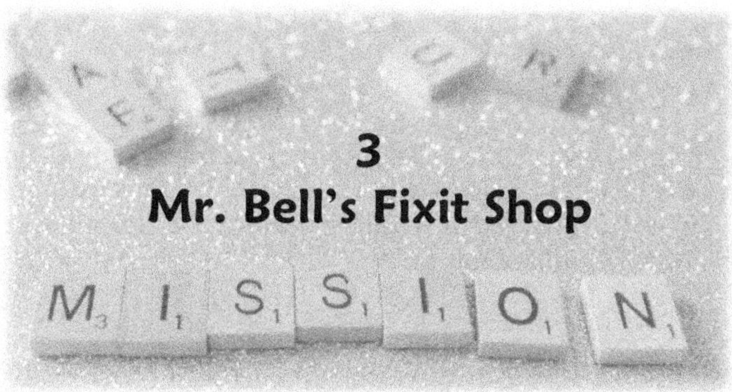

3
Mr. Bell's Fixit Shop

"...The LORD has anointed Me ... to heal the brokenhearted..." (Isaiah 61:1c)

> Mr. Bell could fix almost anything. Broken locks, broken clocks, broken pans, broken fans, broken plates, broken skates—he could fix them all. People smiled when they walked past his little shop and saw the sign in the window. It said: "MR. BELL'S FIXIT SHOP. I FIX EVERYTHING BUT BROKEN HEARTS"—with a picture of a cracked heart.

So begins the story of *Mr. Bell's Fixit Shop* (Ronne Peltzman, 1981)—my children's best-loved Little Golden Book thirty years ago, and now my four-year-old granddaughter's favorite as well. Mr. Bell was a darling septuagenarian who could fix anything and everything that the citizens of his tiny town brought to him. But those qualifications alone don't make for a memorable children's tale.

What elevates the book to a timeless classic—and Mr. Bell to the level of hero—is when Jill, a child who loved to spend her afternoons in his fixit shop, burst through the shop door one day with her favorite doll hopelessly mutilated by the family dog. Our protagonist spends most of the night alone in his shop, applying his near-miraculous fixit powers to the doll's remains. When Jill arrives at the shop next morning, the dolly-love of her life is looking as good—better, even—than when she was new.

"When you fixed my dolly," says Jill, "you fixed my broken heart too." And, in response to the grateful child's urging, Mr. Bell alters the sign in his window: adding a Band-aid over the cracked heart, and changing the words to: "I FIX EVERYTHING—*EVEN* BROKEN HEARTS."

A broken heart is, by definition, a state of grief and despair resulting from the loss of something profoundly meaningful—often a relationship or a person **who is deeply loved**. And the only way to cure a broken heart is either to restore that which was lost (as in the case of Jill), or else to replace it with a new object of profound love, for example, if a child receives a new puppy in place of his beloved dog who died, or a young lady finds true love in place of the weasel who jilted her.

Continuing our fascinating journey through Isaiah 61, the passage prophetic of Jesus' earthly mission, we see Him as the great Healer of broken hearts. He accomplished this feat, of course, through the cross and resurrection—restoring what Adam had lost for us in the Fall: relationship with Him **Who is deeply loved: our Creator**. Through this miracle of reconciliation, He lifted humanity from brokenhearted grief and despair, to the bosom of joy.

But it doesn't end there!

In the story of Mr. Bell, Jill tells him, "I want to have a fixit shop of my own when I grow up." So, Mr. Bell made her his special helper.

While on Earth, Jesus had twelve special helpers. And as He prepared to leave them, He said, "I am sending you, just as the Father has sent Me." (John 20:21 CEV) They had grown up, and now they had a fixit shop of their own. A shop that's come down to you and me.

How do we fix broken hearts? Sure, the power of the gospel—salvation from Sin—is the greatest healer of all. But there are other wounds of the heart as well.

Ezra's commission was the rebuilding of the temple. As the foundation was laid, "Many of the older priests and Levites and family heads, who had seen the former temple, wept aloud when they saw the foundation of the new one being laid, while many others shouted for joy." (Ezra 3:12 NIV) Restoration of worship brought healing to broken hearts.

Nehemiah was sent to the repatriated captives at Jerusalem, who were in a desperate situation of "great distress and reproach" (Nehemiah 1:3) due to their city's wall lying broken and burned. Rebuilding the city wall restored their security, pride, and national identity. The story closes with great joy and celebration (Nehemiah 8) as the people's collective broken heart, now restored, is lifted in praise.

John the Baptist's mission was to "turn heart of the fathers to the children, and the children to their fathers." (Malachi 4:6) Relationships restored. Broken hearts healed.

What has the great Fixer of Broken Hearts ordained **you** to do? Whether the task be great, small, or in-between, you can—as the old hymn says, *"Be His hand extended / Reaching out to the oppressed."*

Why not pray ...

"Dear Father, I know You have a special place for me in the corps of broken-heart healers. Help me discover what it is and, in Your limitless strength, make a difference in the lives of those You place in my path.
In Jesus' name. Amen"

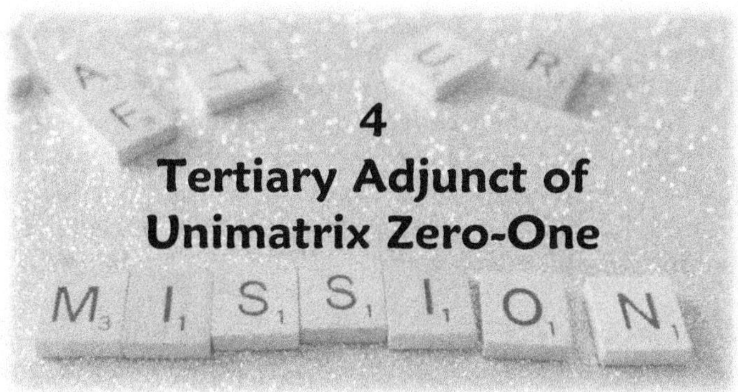

4
Tertiary Adjunct of Unimatrix Zero-One

"...The LORD has anointed Me ... to proclaim freedom for the captives..." (Isaiah 61:1d, NIV)

> "So quiet!" wailed Seven. "Just one voice."
>
> "One voice can be stronger than a thousand voices," replied Janeway. "Your mind is independent now, with its own unique identity."
>
> "You are forcing that identity upon me. It's not mine."
>
> "Oh yes, it is." replied Janeway, her voice brimming with compassion. "I'm just giving you back what was stolen from you. The existence you were denied, the child who never had a chance. That life is yours to live now."

Any serious "Trekkie" would immediately identify this exchange as being from "The Gift"—one of the opening episodes of *Star Trek Voyager's* second season.

"Seven," of course, was short for "Seven of Nine, Tertiary Adjunct of Unimatrix Zero-One"—her Borg designation. Borg have no names, only designations. Names are "irrelevant."

Formerly a human child, Annika Hansen, Seven had been captured and assimilated many years ago by the Borg to become a drone in their collective, where, as half-humanoid-half-machine, their minds are technologically interlinked. Each Borg drone hears the thoughts of the entire collective, so they think and act as one. They find strength and comfort in their communal thought world.

Now, while imprisoned in *Starship Voyager's* brig, as much for her own safety as that of the ship, Seven is unaccustomed to hearing nothing but her own thoughts within her troubled head, rather than thousands of voices. She has been severed from the collective's "hive mind," and the silence is maddening.

It is at this point that Kathryn Janeway, the captain of *Voyager*, meets with Seven and tries to convey the magnitude of the gift of freedom she has been given. But it isn't until the end of the fourth season, about seventy-five episodes later, that Seven finally comes to appreciate her freedom and turns down the opportunity of returning to the Borg collective.

Wherever Jesus walked, we see Him setting captives free. But to effectively continue that ministry—as He commanded us to do—we must be able to recognize captivity in all its manifestations. Moreover, we must understand the addictive effects of long-term captivity on the human mind and spirit.

Captivity can be a source of identity, security, serenity—and torpor. Caught in Satan's web, injected with his mind-numbing venom, the captive feels no compulsion to escape. In fact, even after experiencing new birth through our Savior's blood, it may require months—even years—for many of us Christians to fully yield to the Holy Spirit's venom-purging action.

Captivity has many "perks" that tempt us away from the purposes of God, away from the glorious existence He has ordained for us, away from His promise of "life in abundance."

- The Israelites yearned for the "good old days" of their slavery because the fine cuisine they left behind seemed more enticing than the Promised Land ahead. **Comfort**.

- Or, we have the rich young ruler who couldn't follow the One he recognized as his "Good Master" ... because he would miss the gold clinking in his counting-house. **Wealth**.

- Pilate had repeatedly sought to release Jesus until the Jews played their ace: "If you let this man go, you are no friend of Caesar." Then Pilate washed Jesus off his hands. **Position, power**.

- One disciple would not follow Jesus because he needed to "bury his father"—i.e., he wanted to see the inheritance divided first. **Security**.

- Even Peter, who had been part of Christ's inner circle for more than three years, succumbed to peer pressure around the campfire and denied his Lord. **Fear of man**.

Ponder Jesus' words in Luke 9:23: "If any man would come after Me, let him deny himself, and take up his cross daily, and follow Me."

Herein is the divine paradox: that the cross, which would seem to rob us of freedom, is actually the source of true freedom. "May I never boast," says the Apostle Paul, "except in the cross of our Lord Jesus Christ, through which the world has been crucified to me, and I to the world." (Galatians 6:14, NIV) It is the power of the cross applied daily to our lives that ultimately releases us from the world's grip of captivity—with all its deceptive "perks."

As Captain Janeway explained to Seven of Nine, "I'm just giving you back what was stolen from you. The existence you were denied, the child who never had a chance. That life is yours to live now."

Jesus the Anointed One came to proclaim liberty to the captives. And now He has given us the keys of the Kingdom to go forth and continue the task of setting captives free.

Why not pray ...

"Dear Father, open my eyes to see where I'm still held captive by webs of comfort, entertainment, wealth, security, fear of man, and whatever else. Please set me free, that I may continue Your earthly ministry by proclaiming freedom to all those You send my way.
In Jesus' name. Amen"

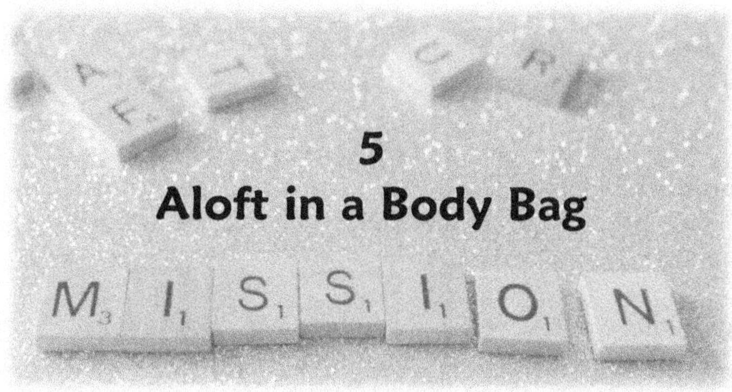

5
Aloft in a Body Bag

"...The LORD has anointed Me ... to proclaim ... release from darkness for the prisoners." (Isaiah 61:1e, NIV)

As the curtain lifts on Chapter 20 of *The Count of Monte Cristo* (Alexandre Dumas, 1844), the protagonist, Edmond Dantès, has been imprisoned fourteen years in the darkest dungeons of the Chateau D'If (a 16th-century French "Alcatraz") after having been framed for a political crime he did not commit. And now, the pious Abbé Faria—who has been Dantès' only dungeon companion, and the only glimmer of hope in his desperate plight—has died, and is lying still in a body bag waiting for the prison guards to come haul him off.

"They will forget me here," laments Dantès in his despair, "and I shall die in my dungeon like Faria.... None but the dead pass freely from this dungeon ..."

At which moment, our hero has an epiphany. Why not bring on death forthwith? And so, he drags his friend's corpse away through a tunnel and stuffs himself into the body bag instead. When the guards show up, they carry him out and launch him off the cliff on which Chateau D'If is perched, and into the sea below—their standard method of burying their hapless dead. Dantès, naturally, had provisioned himself with a knife, so he promptly cut his way out of the body bag and swam off to start his new life as the fabulously rich Count of Monte Cristo. (As for how he came by such fabulous riches ... you will have to read the book.)

By happy accident, our monthly trek through Isaiah 61 brings us on Easter Day to the end of verse one: "The LORD has anointed Me ... to proclaim ... release from darkness for the prisoners..."

In previous weeks, we have sounded the depths of this verse truth by truth, the latest having been "...to proclaim freedom for the captives." We explored various means by which the great enemy of our soul holds his captives in bondage, such as: comfort, entertainment, wealth, security, and the fear of man.

However, it is important to note that our Lord, Whose every word is carefully chosen—He is not given to pointless redundancy—says that He not only came to proclaim "freedom for the captives," but also "release from darkness for the prisoners." Because, not only are there satanic powers that hold us captive to vice, but there are those that would further imprison the soul in the deep darkness of despair. Think of it this way.... If **captivity** is a landslide that blocks our path toward the "life in abundance" our Savior came to gift us, **dark despair** is, by contrast, a Mount Everest landed squarely on top of us, ending all hope of getting there. It is the Chateau D'If, from which dungeon the only way out is in a body bag.

But, just as Abbé Faria provided the only means of escape for Dantès—with his own body bag—our Lord Jesus Christ descended into the grave in order that, through His resurrection, He would set us free from the power of death. And, not only death—which is the ultimate dungeon indeed—but all other dark prisons that confine us. This is, of course, the miracle of Easter.

But what shall we do with this glorious freedom?

Certainly not to imitate Edmond Dantès, who devotes the remainder of his life to exacting revenge from those who sent him to prison those fourteen years. (The Count of Monte Cristo is a bittersweet tale for, without fail, whenever he executes one of his seemingly flawless plots of vengeance, it has the unintended effect of also bringing down sorrow upon those he holds dear ... and, ultimately, on himself.)

What, then? "As the Father has sent me, even so I am sending you," Jesus said. (John 20:21) Which means, among other things, that He is sending us "to proclaim ... release from darkness for the prisoners..."

Jesus never hesitated to go where He could find people bound in darkness. He left the multitudes behind and made a special journey to the country of the Gadarenes just to free a single wretched soul held prisoner by a legion of devils. And, that is not the only one-on-one house call our Lord made. There was the Samaritan woman, a lonely outcast of five shipwrecked marriages. And the widow of Nain, who had lost her only son and hope of provision.

As we reflect on our Lord's incomprehensible love, which sprung us from Satan's dungeon by means of His own body bag, to the glorious new life of Easter morning, let us not lose sight of His compelling commission in Isaiah 61. "As the Father has sent me, even so I am sending you."

Why not pray ...

"Dear Father, thank you for Jesus. Thank you for His death and resurrection that set me free, not only from the darkness of sin and death, but also from the many dark prisons in which the enemy would confine me. Please give me a passion to continue Jesus' ministry of setting free those who are oppressed by the devil. And, by Your power I shall!
In Jesus' name. Amen"

6
Peace, Beaver!

"...The LORD has anointed Me ... to proclaim the year of the LORD's favor ..." (Isaiah 61:1-2a, NIV)

> One of the leopards approached Aslan and said, "Sire, there is a messenger from the enemy who craves audience."
>
> "Let him approach," said Aslan. The leopard went away and soon returned leading the Witch's dwarf.
>
> "What is your message, Son of Earth?" asked Aslan.
>
> "The Queen of Narnia and Empress of the Lone Islands desires a safe conduct to come and speak with you," said the dwarf, "on a matter which is as much to your advantage as to hers."
>
> "Queen of Narnia, indeed!" said Mr. Beaver. "Of all the cheek ..."
>
> "Peace, Beaver," said Aslan. "All names will soon be restored to their proper owners."
>
> (From *The Lion, the Witch, and the Wardrobe* [1950]. Chapter 13. C.S. Lewis.)

My most cherished stories—books and movies—have always been the classics. But especially those featuring the displaced protagonist in a long and bitter struggle to reclaim what is rightfully his (or hers). This formula was especially popular with nineteenth-century novelists, handing us many exceptional tales such as:

- *Ben Hur*, by Lew Wallace (1880)
- *The Prince and the Pauper*, by Mark Twain (1881)
- *Kidnapped*, by Robert Louis Stevenson (1886)
- *The Prisoner of Zenda*, by Anthony Hope Hawkins (1894)

Of course, C.S. Lewis's allegory *The Lion, the Witch, and the Wardrobe* was based on a true story ... the greatest of all time ... which was Jesus' coming to Earth to reclaim what was rightfully His—the human race. Just as the white witch, Jadis, had illegitimately crowned herself "Queen of Narnia" and oppressed Aslan's people, our enemy of old, Satan, fashioned himself "Ruler of Earth," confiscating all that belonged to God's children: life, liberty, happiness ... everything.

We have hung out for many weeks in the opening verse of Isaiah 61, where Jesus (in His Luke 4 reading) announces His ministry to free the poor, the brokenhearted, the bound, and the desperate.

But He doesn't stop there, hallelujah! He goes on to tell what these newly freed captives will **reclaim**.

See, Jesus' audience that day had no trouble understanding what was meant by "to proclaim the year of the LORD's favor." It is a clear reference to the Levitical Year of Jubilee—when slaves must be released to their rightful life of freedom, and when properties must be released to revert to their rightful owners.

"And you shall consecrate the fiftieth year, and proclaim liberty throughout all the land to all its inhabitants. It shall be a Jubilee for you; and each of you shall return to his possession, and each of you shall return to his family." (Leviticus 25:10)

It was so named "the Year of Jubilee," not because it was to last for just one year, after which all those slaves could be recaptured and properties seized once again. NO, rather, it was the year when all those people and properties should become—in the words of Abraham Lincoln's Emancipation Proclamation—"then, thenceforward, and forever free." Or, as Aslan put it, it was the year when "all names [would] ... be restored to their proper owners."

The Apostle John writes, "Behold what manner of love the Father has bestowed on us, that we should be called children of God!" (I John 3:1a)

And Peter: "Once you were nobody. Now you are God's people." (I Peter 2:10a, CEV)

As the Jews sing at Passover, "Dayenu!"—meaning, "It would have been enough!"—if God had just set us free from Egypt. But He has done so much more. Whereas Isaiah 61:1 is the Red Sea crossing out of captivity, verse 2 is the Jordan crossing into the promised land. Where verse 1 springs us from the "Queen of Narnia's" prison, verse 2 restores us to our rightful place from the dawn of creation—as God's own people. Not just for one blessed year, but henceforth and forever. Amen.

Once again, let's remember that Jesus started this whole Isaiah 61 / Luke 4 ministry ... just to hand us the reins. "Just as the Father has sent Me, I also send you." (John 20:21b, NASB)

Why not pray ...

"Dear Father, thank you for Your amazing grace, which not only freed me from sin, but also restored me to my rightful

inheritance as a child of God! Let me never lose sight of my commission, but rather light within me an ever-increasing flame of passion to carry on Your ministry of modeling and proclaiming the Isaiah 61 message of deliverance and reconciliation to all those You send my way.
In Jesus' name. Amen"

7
Truman's Beard and The Clock Strikes Twelve

"...The LORD has anointed Me ... to proclaim ... the day of vengeance of our God..." (Isaiah 61:1-2b)

In Mike Beard's own words, "How many times can you interview the same subject, even if he's Harry Truman...?"

Beard was the lone reporter assigned to cover scientific happenings around Mount St. Helens during the cold spring of 1980. "It wasn't the most glamorous assignment," he says in retrospect. "It was an hourlong round-trip drive from Portland; not much was happening other than the earthquake swarms, and I wasn't the only reporter quickly running out of fresh story ideas." But then there was Truman....

Harry R. Truman—*No, he was* ***not*** *named after our 33rd president*—was a crusty octogenarian World War I veteran, Prohibition bootlegger, prospector, pink-Cadillac owner, and 50-years proprietor of a magnificent mountain lodge at Spirit Lake.

As March wore on and geologists' warnings intensified, everyone abandoned the mountain—property owners, residents, campers, thrill-seekers. Everyone, that is, except Truman. When one of the tremors knocked him out of bed at night, he simply moved his mattress to the cellar. "The mountain's a mile away, and it ain't gonna hurt me!" he said.

State officials and other emissaries showed up at Harry's lodge. "That mountain is a giant clock," they said. "No one knows when it will strike twelve; but when it does, your number's up!" They tried ordering him to leave, reasoning with him, imploring him. But none was as persistent as Mike Beard. Plying his skill a newsman, Beard pressed the old curmudgeon with his most persuasive arguments in the form of interview questions, but still nothing could sway him. On the contrary, Truman seemed to enjoy his new stardom—as the news articles resulted in stacks of fan mail ... even marriage proposals.

Until May 18, 1980 ... when Mount St. Helens struck twelve. Harry R. Truman, folk hero and mountain man, became part of his beloved mountain ... instantaneously buried, lodge and all, under 150 feet of volcanic material.

So far, we have been following the epic Messianic prophecy that is Isaiah 61. To launch His public ministry, Jesus took the synagogue podium in His hometown of Nazareth, unfurled the Isaiah scroll, and read from chapter 61: just the first two verses, nothing more. As a matter of fact, He stopped mid-sentence in verse two: "...The LORD has anointed Me ... to proclaim the year of the LORD's favor..." Then He sat down, never finishing the thought: "... and [to proclaim] the day of our God's vengeance."

But, why?

According to the Gospels, Jesus' earthly message could be summed up in a single sentence: "Repent, for the Kingdom of Heaven is at hand!" He was here to proclaim—to announce—what was about to take place when the King of the Universe, God Almighty, would start the great clock of the Messianic Age of Grace through Jesus' death, burial, and resurrection.

But what about the "day of our God's vengeance"? Did Jesus just invalidate, or at least gloss over, the portentous and much-alluded-to "Day of the Lord"—when He Himself should sit in judgment at the end of the age? What's up with that?

Actually, no mystery here. As the wise author of Ecclesiastes reminds us, "There is a time for everything, and a season for every activity under the heavens." See, it wasn't Jesus' moment to announce the end of an age that had not yet begun, the striking of a clock that had not yet begun to tick. Rather, His message that day, and throughout His three-plus-years of earthly ministry, was the Amazing Grace soon to be available through His own shed blood. Hallelujah!

Jesus Himself clarified what His ministry was, and wasn't, focused on. A couple of examples:

"For God did not send his Son into the world to condemn the world, but to save the world through him." (John 3:17, NIV)

"If anyone hears my words but does not keep them, I do not judge that person. For I did not come to judge the world, but to save the world. There is a judge for the one who rejects me and does not accept my words; the very words I have spoken will condemn them at the last day." (John 12:47-48, NIV)

Who, then, will sound the warning about the day of judgment?

Yet again, we are reminded of Jesus' commission: "Just as the Father has sent Me, I also send you." (John 20:21b, NASB)

But in this case, we've been ordained not only to continue His ministry that began with the first verse-and-a-half of Isaiah 61, but the whole rest of the chapter as well—including warning our world about the coming Day of the Lord.

Beginning with the very first apostolic sermon—Peter's, in Acts 2—we hear the message loud and clear of the "... coming of the great and glorious day of the Lord," and the call to "Repent..." as "...with many other words he warned them...."

Paul echoed the warning, for example, when he admonished Governor Felix about the "judgment to come" (Acts 24:25). And in his Mars Hill sermon: "In the past God overlooked such ignorance, but now he commands all people everywhere to repent. For he has set a day when he will judge the world with justice by the man he has appointed. He has given proof of this to everyone by raising him from the dead." (Acts 17:30-31, NIV)

The Age of Messianic Grace is ticking away and, when it strikes twelve, it will be a "doomsday clock" indeed for those who have spurned their Savior's love. Tragically, Harry R. Truman is alive and well today—living next door, walking the halls of government, teaching in our schools and universities: "The mountain's a mile away, and it ain't gonna hurt us, nohow!" But, as God's grace would have it, for every Truman there is a Mike Beard.

Why not pray ...

"Dear Father, thank you that You so loved the world as to send Your precious Son to save us from ourselves. Cause me to feel Your urgency for a world that's closer to its Day of Vengeance with every tick of the clock. In whatever capacity You have set me, by Your Holy Spirit anointing, and—like Mike Beard—by means of whatever skills and giftings You have endowed me with, please help me communicate Your gospel of love to those who need to hear.
In Jesus' name. Amen"

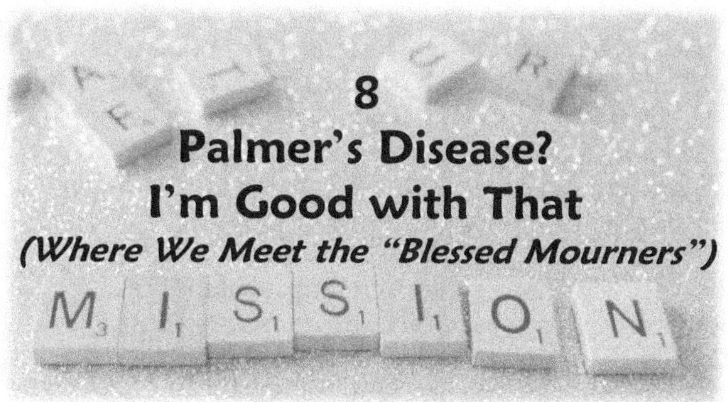

8
Palmer's Disease? I'm Good with That
(Where We Meet the "Blessed Mourners")

"... To comfort all who mourn, to console those who mourn in Zion ..." (Isaiah 61:2c-3a)

> "Why should I believe that life up there in your world is any better than life down here on *Goliath*?" said McKenzie, "... You know, I can't help feeling that if a spaceship were to land upon Earth from another planet and aliens said to the people, 'We have come to rescue you,' the answer might be, 'Rescue us? From what?'"

Now, if that isn't a novel thought...!

But, in case you don't recognize the memorable quote, it's from the B movie "Goliath Awaits" (Columbia Pictures Television, 1981). The fiction flick is about the *Goliath*, an ocean liner much longer than the *Titanic*, sunk by Nazi torpedoes in 1939 and discovered by divers 40 years later ... with more than 300 survivors still aboard!

But when the rescue expedition arrives, as described in the original movie blurb: "The big problem is not bringing them to the surface ... but convincing their leader to let them go!" See, living in the crumbling hulk of a ship, where life support systems were failing and people were dying of "Palmer's disease" (a malady that mysteriously dispatched its victims—usually the elderly, the weak, or the injured—within minutes) was an okay existence for some ... such as their megalomaniac leader Paul McKenzie, the henchmen who helped create and maintain his "special world," and some of the younger generation who knew no other reality.

In the face of violent opposition and sabotage, the protagonists were ultimately able to isolate those who lamented their ghastly estate and set them free. (It's actually well worth the watch! Hint: YouTube.)

Continuing our Isaiah 61 adventure, we come to the part of our Savior's job description where He "comforts all who mourn." In fact, not only does He promise to comfort these mourners, but He actually seems to commend them: "Blessed are those who mourn, for they shall be comforted." (Matthew 5:4)

But ... why "blessed"? On the contrary, when I think of "one who mourns," I picture a moody, self-pitiful, peevish little boy whose uncle "comforts" him by tossing a nickel, saying, "Go buy yourself a pack of gum and get out of my hair!" Sort of a backhanded blessing, right?

But the Isaiah 61 "those who mourn" crowd aren't doleful little people. Rather, they are profoundly grieved by all that is unjust, tragic, and deplorable. Think of the prophet Jeremiah's lamentations ... in the book by that name. Think of creation itself that "groans and travails" (Romans 8:22) because of the sinful state of this world. Think of someone you know who is so appalled by injustice, crushed by oppression, or doubled over in empathy for another's pain as to say, "I can't take this anymore!"

NOW you've found the "Blessed Mourner" that Jesus came to comfort! Not the old Paul McKenzie in love with his "special world" of sin because, though it's crashing down around his ears, at least he's still at the center of it. Not the woke young person parroting "tolerance, diversity, and peace" while watching friends, family, and society spinning down the toilet.

Jesus said, "I did not come to call the [self-proclaimed] righteous [who see no need to repent], but sinners to repentance...." (Luke 5:32, AMP)

As we continue Jesus' work on Earth—"Just as the Father has sent Me, I also send you." (John 20:21b, NASB)—let's be on the lookout for those "Blessed Mourners."

Why not pray ...

"Dear Father, help me go through life with my eyes open. Help me recognize the souls that Your Holy Spirit has softened up to where they're crying out, 'I can't take it anymore!' And then, with the holy boldness I get from a whispered prayer [see Nehemiah 2], help me open not only my heart, but also my mouth, to say, 'I'm going to pray for you because I can attest to the fact that God cares, He listens, and He can both comfort AND rescue you!'
In Jesus' name. Amen"

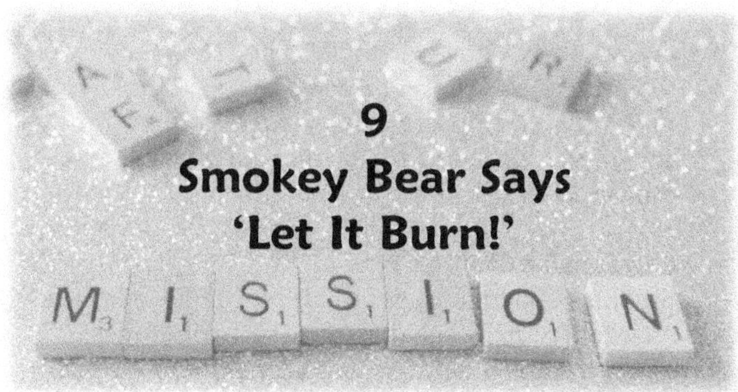

9
Smokey Bear Says 'Let It Burn!'

"... The LORD has anointed Me ... To console those who mourn in Zion, to give them beauty for ashes ..." (Isaiah 61:1b-3b)

Smokey Bear. More American than Thanksgiving turkey or Casey at the Bat, at 79 years and counting, Smokey Bear is the longest-running PSA (public service announcement).

Time for some Smokey trivia ...

- **Most recognizable mug:** According to the American Ad Council, the source of PSAs, Smokey Bear's image was correctly identified, and the ad campaign messages recognized, by 80% of "outdoor recreationists."

- **No middle name**: By solemn act of Congress (The Smokey Bear Act of 1952), his name was established as "Smokey Bear"—NOT "Smokey The Bear."

- **Alive before he was born**: We've all heard how Smokey Bear (as a cub) was rescued from a forest fire and came to live at the National Zoo in Washington, D.C.—where he became the living mascot for fire safety. The truth, however, is that the U.S. Forest Service's first Smokey Bear campaign poster was issued in 1944—fully six years before our little cub was rescued from the Capitan Gap Fire in New Mexico.

- **His family**: While living at the National Zoo, Smokey Bear had a wife named Goldie Bear and an adopted son (because they were childless) whose name was Little Smokey.

- **His own ZIP Code**: That's right! By 1964, Smokey Bear was receiving so much fan mail—over 1800 pieces per day—that the U.S. Postal Service had to assign him his own ZIP Code: 20252.

- **But saddest of all**: During his 26 long years on Earth, Smokey Bear only learned to say one thing: "Remember ... only YOU can prevent forest fires." But it turns out ... he was *wrong* about forest fires! Read on and find out why.

On our last Isaiah 61 visit, we met a new breed—the Blessed Mourners—who are so appalled by the ravishes of sin on the people, the nation, and the world they love that they are moved to weeping, prayer, and decisive action. Jesus came, not only to comfort these Mourners, but to shape them into a new world order—His Kingdom order. And, in fact, the rest of the chapter is a playbook for how He makes that happen.

But verse 3 is all about how He **comforts** them. And where does this comfort begin? "Beauty for ashes."

"Ah, yes! A pleasant thought," you say? No. Read it again. "Beauty for ashes. Beauty **for ashes**." It's a trade: to get His beauty requires **our ashes first**.

This "**ashes first**" thing is a perennial truth. A Kingdom law with no exceptions and no shortcuts. If I sincerely desire life in abundance—in all its fullness, shimmering with all the **beauty** of His purposes made perfect in me—then I must be ready for the part where my own schemes and dreams get reduced to **ashes**.

Which leads to an uncomfortable thought!... Just as, "Where there's smoke, there's fire" ... "Where there's **ashes**, there has surely been **fire**!" And **fire** means **death**. Death, not only of my schemes and dreams, but—get this!—death, even, of my human efforts toward becoming the person God needs me to be. It must all be tried by fire, leading to death, leading to **ashes**. And yet, ashes now is better than ashes later!

"Each one's work will become clear; for the Day will declare it, because it will be revealed by fire; and the fire will test each one's work, of what sort it is. If anyone's work which he has built on it endures, he will receive a reward. If anyone's work is burned, he will suffer loss; but he himself will be saved, yet so as through fire." (1 Corinthians 3:13-15)

So, I have a choice: submit to God's plan of **fire**, **death**, **ashes** during my lifetime ... resulting in His true **beauty** blossoming forth in my life; or else skip all that uncomfortable stuff and muddle through on my own efforts. In the latter case, sure, I may still pass "the [Judgment] Day's" fire test, but I'll be left standing there naked and ashamed. What it really comes down to, then, is "ashes now, with an abundant life of God's **beauty,** or ashes later with nothing to show for it but **regrets**."

All of which brings us back to the gospel according to Smokey Bear: "Remember ... only YOU can prevent forest fires." Interestingly, the Ad Council realized that Smokey's message was misfiring, and they quietly amended it in 2001 to be: "Remember ... only YOU can prevent **wildfires**." See, ever since the 1940s, Smokey and his friends—especially Bambi, who was another Forest Service spokesman—had burned into our consciousness the images of **forest fires**, set by **Man**, destroying innocent woodlands and the creatures that live there. Evil. Evil. ***EVIL!***

However, modern forest conservation science was quickly learning that forest fires can be beneficial. No, not the wildfires set by arsonists or accidentally kindled by careless campers. But controlled burns, whether initiated by nature or by human hands, are both helpful and essential to maintain healthy woodlands. Take Yellowstone National Park, for example. NPS.gov tells the story:

> Fire suppression in Yellowstone began with the arrival of the U.S. Army, which was placed in charge of protecting the park in 1886. The Army, which was in Yellowstone until 1918, successfully extinguished some fires in the belief that suppression would help save the forests.... Records indicate fire was almost completely excluded (suppressed) from the Douglas-fir, sagebrush steppe, and aspen communities on the northern range from 1886 until 1987.
>
> By the 1940s, ecologists recognized fire was a natural and unavoidable change agent in many ecosystems... In the 1950s and 1960s, other parks and forests began to experiment with controlled burns. In 1972 ... two backcountry areas in [Yellowstone] park totaling 340,000 acres ... were designated as locations where natural fires could burn. After three years, during which 10 fires burned a total of 831 acres in the two natural fire zones, the non-suppression area was expanded to include most of the park.... From 1972 to 1987, 235 fires were allowed to burn 33,759 acres in Yellowstone.

But the average Joe and Jane American were left scratching their heads. How could the U.S. Forest Service be flouting the advice of their very own expert, Smokey Bear?

All of us must be open to new learning, even Smokey Bear,

whose message finally changed in 2001 (posthumously, it would seem) to focus on wildfires, rather than forest fires in general. He learned that nature's law of forestry includes periodic forest fires, either set by lightning or intentionally by man, for a number of very good reasons:

- Clearing dead trees, underbrush, and leaves from the forest floor so new vegetation can emerge
- Allowing more sunlight through
- Returning nutrients (as ashes) to the forest topsoil
- Aiding certain trees that actually **require fire** in order to release their seeds, such as the lodgepole pine.

Scripture gives us numerous examples of heroes of faith whose prophetic vision of God's plan for them first had to be reduced to ashes before it could emerge in its full beauty. Think of Abraham, Jacob, Moses, and David. Or, how about Joseph? Remember those splendid dreams, where his brothers were falling prostrate before him? Actually, they **did** bow to him later, but not before he had been roughed up, cast into a pit and left for dead, sold as a slave to an alien land, falsely accused of a crime and locked up in prison. Talk about ashes! But, on close examination, each account reveals a deeply flawed human who had to run the gauntlet of adversity, seeing all his dreams and schemes reduced to ashes, before God could use him.

Hear Jesus' call today: "O Blessed Mourner! I treasure your heart of prayer and zeal for the Kingdom. Come join My army. Take My yoke upon you and learn of Me. I'll make a man (or woman) out of you! Come experience **death** ... **ashes** ... and finally My **beauty** as rivers of living water flow from you to a thirsty world!"

Why not pray ...

"Dear Father, help me live each day in perspective of "that Day." I don't want to enter Heaven with my tail between my legs, having relied on my own plans and efforts, only to see them burnt to ash at the last Judgment. Please bring on the fire, death, and ashes ***now****, so Your beauty can burst forth as the seed of the lodgepole pine—a tree of righteousness in your Kingdom's fine woodland!'*
In Jesus' name. Amen"

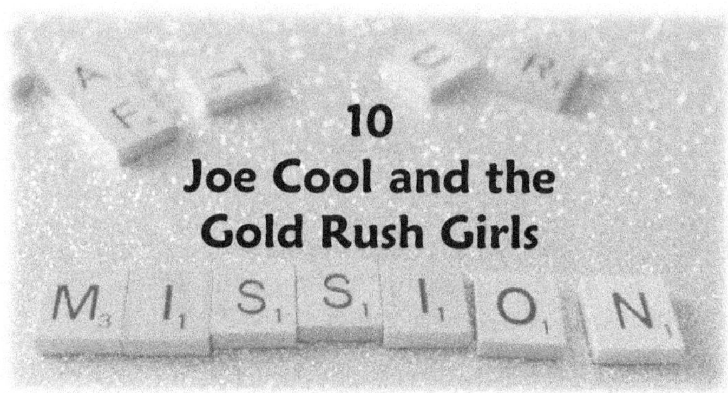

10
Joe Cool and the Gold Rush Girls

"... The LORD has anointed Me ... To console those who mourn in Zion, to give them ... the oil of joy for mourning..." (Isaiah 61:1b-3c)

So [King David] got the Covenant Box from Obed's house to take it to Jerusalem with a great celebration. After the men carrying the Covenant Box had gone six steps, David had them stop while he offered the Lord a sacrifice of a bull and a fattened calf. David, wearing only a linen cloth around his waist, danced with all his might to honor the Lord. And so he and all the Israelites took the Covenant Box up to Jerusalem with shouts of joy and the sound of trumpets.

As the Box was being brought into the city, Michal, Saul's daughter, looked out of the window and saw King David dancing and jumping around in the sacred dance, and she was disgusted with him. Afterward, when David went home to greet his family, Michal came out to meet him. "The king of Israel made a big name for himself today!" she said. "He exposed himself like a fool in the sight of the servant women of his officials!"

David answered, "I was dancing to honor the Lord, who chose me instead of your father and his family to make me the leader of his people Israel. And I

> will go on dancing to honor the Lord, and will disgrace myself even more."
>
> (2 Samuel 6:12b-22, GNT, excerpts)

To fully appreciate what was going on in King David's head, we first need to rewind about three months, where there's quite a different scene being played out.

The "Covenant Box"— the Ark of the Covenant—had been captured in battle quite some time ago by Israel's archenemies, the Philistines, who had then reluctantly given it back after God struck them with a plague. Since then, it had been sitting in a sort of prolonged quarantine at Abinadab's house, while Israel went through a period of mourning and licking their wounds.

What King David needed was a morale-booster event, and he knew just the thing. He would be *The One Who Brought Back the Box!* He'd lead a pompous procession to outshine all other pompous processions ... ushering the Covenant Box back to its rightful place in Jerusalem. So, David had convened 30,000 noble men for the occasion, along with a marching orchestra with himself at the head—most likely playing the finest of instruments, and most likely singing, in four-part harmony, ceremonious psalms that he himself had written for the occasion—as he solemnly led the procession from Abinadab's house.

To make a long story short ... well, in fact, God did make the long story short! The somber procession which, though well intentioned, was both illegal and ill-conceived, quickly came to a tragic end. In His eternal righteousness, God was forced to cut it short with a lightning bolt from heaven, resulting in the death of one of Abinadab's sons, Uzzah, who was driving the ox-cart.

Ox-cart??

Yeah, that was the illegal part: because God's Law strictly laid out the method for transporting His holy Covenant Box. It was to be borne by the priestly class, not the beastly class. But ill-conceived? Though a bit more subtle, King David "got it." See, his morale-booster event was all about **him**—David—leading **his** procession, leading **his** music, with the Covenant Box meekly following the oxen back to its assigned place in **his** capital.

But something snapped in King David's brain (and heart) that day. Call it a God-snap ... something like that white-hot lightning bolt he'd witnessed! And **now**, fast-forward three months later, and he was ready to try this thing again. To get it **right** this time!

"The LORD has anointed Me ... To console those who mourn in Zion, to give them ... the oil of joy for mourning." That's our Lord's own heart for his people, and that's the heart we see in David when it comes time for the Parade Sequel, in 2 Samuel chapter 6, starting at verse 12—this time bringing up the Covenant Box from Obed's house instead of Abinadab's.

He'd come to realize that it wasn't all about David himself, but about God Himself. Yes, the idea of a morale-booster was born in his heart by God Himself. God was turning Israel's page from the failed reign of King Saul to a new beginning with David. From oppression to praise. From **mourning** to **joy**.

This called, not for a solemn procession, but a wild parade! God was figuratively bringing back the captivity of Israel, breaking the yoke of the Philistines from their neck, and turning their mourning into dancing! Sure, there was music this time, but it was music you could really rock to.

And rock they all did! Back to our lead-in Scripture, we now see David rocking it out in front of them all, not seeking to make himself the hero, but rather wildly praising God—the true Hero of the day. Cross-referencing details of this event in 1 Chronicles chapter 16, we understand that David started the parade wearing a fine royal robe, but as things got joyfully hot, he shed the robe and continued with just a linen cloth around his waist, whirling, leaping, and shouting joyful praises to Almighty God, Who had delivered His Covenant Box, and His people, from their mourning.

To grasp the impact of King David's un-kingly behavior—which left his wife (Saul's daughter) horror-stricken as she observed the parade from the security of her window—think of "Joe Cool" Montana, greatest of the great, the impeccably-mannered quarterback, ready to throw his historic pass against the Cowboys in January 1982. Montana lines up at the five ... on third down and three ... He's got the ball! Montana rolls right, looking, looking to throw! NFL history is about to be made....

But then, as the crowd holds its collective breath in bated anticipation, Joe looks up and ... *something snaps*. He drops the ball carelessly on the field, sprints over to where the Gold Rush Girls are standing, strips down to his boxers and tee shirt, and leads them in a wild sequence of cheers for the crowd, cheers for the teams, cheers for the love of Football!

You're probably thinking by now how we've strayed a long way from the topic of Isaiah 61. But think again! Our Lord Jesus was anointed "... to console those who mourn in Zion, to give them ... the oil of joy for mourning..." It's **He** Who came to turn the page. It's **He** Who came to die and atone for our mournful state of Sin, to rise again, and to ascend to the Father's right hand, where He ever lives to make intercession for us. Hallelujah! If that doesn't call for stripping off our three-piece suits and dancing in joy and worship in our undies!... (Well, you get the point. And maybe your "secret prayer closet" is the place for such exalted worship.)

Christianity is not about church, not about the worship band, nor the choir ... not even about the sermon. (Horrors! Dare we say that?) It's all about Jesus Christ, King of the Universe, Deliverer of His people.

Why not pray ...

"Dear Father, thank you for Jesus' triumph over Sin, the Grave, and Mourning. Thank you that—as 2 Corinthians 2:14 says, 'Christ always leads us in triumphal procession, and through us spreads the fragrance of the knowledge of Him everywhere.' Please help me respond with abandon, with a dancing heart to honor the Lord and 'disgrace myself' even more, as King David did, to spread the oil of joy to those around me, and so continue the Isaiah 61 work of my Lord Christ.
In Jesus' name. Amen"

11
Horsie Rides with Haman

"... The LORD has anointed Me ... To console those who mourn in Zion, to give them ... the garment [mantle, cloak] of praise for [instead of] the spirit of heaviness [grief, fainting, despair]..." (Isaiah 61:1b-3d)

When Haman entered, the king asked him, "What should be done for the man the king delights to honor?"

Now Haman thought to himself, "Who is there that the king would rather honor than *me?"* So he answered the king, "For the man the king delights to honor, have them bring a royal robe the king has worn and a horse the king has ridden, one with a royal crest placed on its head. Then let the robe and horse be entrusted to one of the king's most noble princes. Let them robe the man the king delights to honor, and lead him on the horse through the city streets, proclaiming before him, 'This is what is done for the man the king delights to honor!'"

"Go at once," the king commanded Haman. "Get the robe and the horse and do just as you have suggested for Mordecai the Jew, who sits at the king's gate. Do not neglect anything you have recommended."

So Haman got the robe and the horse. He robed Mordecai, and led him on horseback through the

> city streets, proclaiming before him, "This is what is done for the man the king delights to honor!"
>
> Afterward Mordecai returned to the king's gate. But Haman rushed home, with his head covered in grief, and told Zeresh his wife and all his friends everything that had happened to him.
>
> His advisers and his wife Zeresh said to him, "Since Mordecai, before whom your downfall has started, is of Jewish origin, you cannot stand against him—you will surely come to ruin!"
>
> (Esther 6:6-13, NIV)

Today's Isaiah 61 devotional comes direct from Holy Scripture's grandest "fairy tale" love story—complete with handsome young king, scumbag villain, and lowly damsel who becomes queen through a series of serendipitous events. The best part is that it all happened in **real life**—a treasure box of allegory and inspiration from the pages of Bible history.

But what makes this particular scene from the Book of Esther most poignant is its backstory. Mordecai's niece—now the grand Queen Esther of Persia—had him mobilize the city's entire Jewish population to three days of affliction, fasting, and prayer against Haman's murderous extermination plan ... a plan that would not stop at the palace gate, but would include the death of the queen herself, since she was a Jew.

The king, of course, was blissfully oblivious to all of this when he ordered his trusty minister to parade Mordecai the Jew through the streets of the capital, wearing the king's own cloak and seated on his royal steed. (Oh say, can you say ... "irony"?)

But, how does this relate to Isaiah 61?

As our Lord Jesus made known in his great inaugural

speech—Luke chapter 4 (quoting from Isaiah 61)—He was anointed and sent forth by the Father to rescue those Blessed Mourners (that's us!) who lament the sinful state of mankind and afflict their souls in prayer to see His saving hand. And one of the first things He'll do? Give them "the mantle of praise" in exchange for their heaviness and grief.

What does this look like?

Think of a time when you were alarmed by a news story or appalled by a revelation on social media. When you felt the needle of disgust, grief, and—yes, despair—stab deep into your gut or, as it says in Acts 2:37, you were "pricked to the heart." I mean, to the point where your jaw went unhinged and your knees went limp with heaviness and grief ... and all you could think was, "God, how can this be?" And, "God, **please** ... **do** something!" (Remember September 11?)

As Nehemiah reacted, when he was first apprised of the desperate conditions under which the repatriated captives in Jerusalem were living: "I sat weeping and mourning for **days**, and I continued fasting and praying before the God of heaven." (Nehemiah 1:4) Or, as Ezra the Priest reacted when they told him how quickly the people had backslidden into sin with their idolatrous neighbors: "When I heard this, I tore my tunic and cloak, pulled hair from my head and beard and sat down appalled." (Ezra 9:3) Or, as Mordecai reacted in today's passage from the Book of Esther, wrapping himself in sackcloth and leading the Jews of Shushan in three days of desperate appeal to God for their lives ...

When you have that sort of a Nehemiah moment—Ezra moment—Mordecai moment—**that's** when you know you've joined the ranks of the Blessed Mourners. **That's** when you've become a mighty intercessory hammer in the Master's hand. The kind that is "made powerful by God to tear down strongholds" (2 Corinthians 10:4) in prayer.

And it's from the very womb of that gripping backstory that the transcendent episode of today's passage is birthed.

Picture Mordecai, still swathed in sackcloth, passed out on the floor after three days of passionate prayer and fasting. And at sunrise, a knock on the door—his archnemesis, Haman! Who proceeds to clothe him in the king's own mantle, set him on the king's horse, and herald him all through the city as "the man the king delights to honor!" (And the true spectacle here was not Mordecai, but Haman—humiliated beyond recovery, as his own wife and advisers were quick to point out upon his return home.)

Unspeakable joy! ... and, incidentally, a profound allegory of the dawn of the Messianic Age almost five centuries later. After three days in the valley of grief and impending death, Mordecai is wrapped in the king's own mantle—symbolic of the king's delight. After three days in the tomb, Christ arose victorious, making a public spectacle of principalities and powers, so that—**in Him**, wrapped in the mantle of His Spirit—we too, may burst forth to joyous abundant life.

Now, as we continue Jesus' work on Earth—"Just as the Father has sent Me, I also send you" (John 20:21b, NASB)—let's employ all the mighty tools He's equipped us with, **including** the "mantle of praise in exchange for heaviness." It's a powerful cloak of transcendent joy, reserved for the Blessed Mourners, who have obtained it **only** in exchange for heaviness—grief, fainting, and desperate intercessory pursuit of God.

As the psalmist said, "He who continually goes forth weeping, bearing seed for sowing, shall doubtless come again with rejoicing, bringing his sheaves with him." (Psalms 126:6)

Why not pray ...

"Dear Father, I thank You for calling me to take up Your yoke, to share Your intercessory heart for a lost and dying world. So, whatever specific yoke You have for me ***today****, please lay it on me thick! And help me bear it faithfully and fervently, so I'll be worthy to exchange it tomorrow for Your glorious mantle of joy.*
In Jesus' name. Amen"

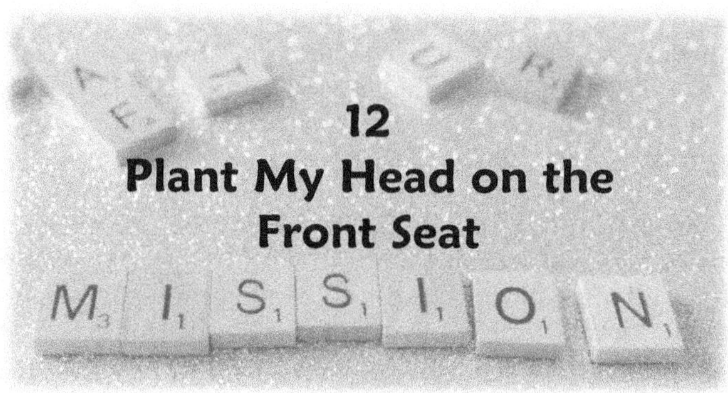

12
Plant My Head on the Front Seat

"... The LORD has anointed Me ... To console those who mourn in Zion ... That they may be called trees of righteousness, the planting of the Lord, that He may be glorified." (Isaiah 61:1b-3e)

> I remember another experience I used to have in Atlanta. I went to high school on the other side of town—to the Booker T. Washington High School.... In those days, rigid patterns of segregation existed on the buses, so that Negroes had to sit in the backs of buses.... I would end up having to go to the back of that bus with my body, but every time I got on that bus, I left my mind up on the front seat. And I said to myself, "One of these days, I'm going to put my body up there where my mind is."
>
> (From *The Autobiography of Martin Luther King, Jr.* [excerpts], © 1998 by The Heirs to the Estate of Martin Luther King, Jr.)

By happy coincidence, just as we're crossing into a new year [2022] at the time of this writing, our journey through Isaiah 61, the "Messianic Playbook," turns a corner as well. In fact, whenever roads appear to intersect in time and eternity, God's people are called to "lift up [our] heads, awake out of sleep" (Luke 21:28, Rom. 13:11-12), for the breath of God may be blowing afresh. His desire is for us to "understand the times, and what [we] should do" (1 Chronicles 12:32). So, let's consider what God may be saying to us ... you and me, **personally** ... at this juncture.

In review: Jesus' earthly ministry, which He launched on the first two verses of Isaiah 61, began with His broad redemptive plan for all of mankind. But it didn't stop there, as we've seen already. Verse 3 shifts the focus to a very special group, the Blessed Mourners, the soil of whose hearts has been tenderized by tears on account of the ravages of sin they witness all around them, to the point that ... well, things begin to happen!

As the Gospel seed germinates gloriously within the mourner's heart, it first brings "comfort, beauty, joy, and praise" (which we've observed in the latest four devotional segments). But there's no stopping it now! Turn the corner, and behold! Verse 3 concludes with a monument to God's handiwork that cannot be missed: Where the seed fell, there now stands a "tree of righteousness" for all to see, an unmistakable work of God to the glory of His name. Hallelujah!

Hmmm ... OK, but just what does that mean? Poetic hyperbole?

Not at all. First, think of a **tree** ... sprung from a **seed**. Now, there's nothing as prophetic as a seed. Within its little body there are three crucial elements: life, character, and connection. Meaning, it's every bit as alive as the tree that will grow from it ("life"), and it knows precisely how to grow itself into that tree—every wrinkle of the bark, every branch crotch, every leaf node—is all pre-programmed into the tiny seed's DNA ("character").

And yet, as Jesus said in John 12:24, the seed must "die" before it can become a fruit-bearing tree. And that's where "connection" comes in. That little seed knows how to respond and interact with the moisture and temperature of the soil around it, by splitting open and launching itself forth as a new creation, connecting with air, water, and soil nutrients to produce what we call **fruit**. That is, a product beneficial to the world in which it exists.

Back to us, the "trees of righteousness." What sort of *fruit* would you expect from such a tree? Why, *righteousness*, of course. Now, unfortunately, that's not a word we use much in our generation. To put it in modern vernacular, "righteousness" is really "justice," but on steroids—enriched with moral and spiritual goodness, which transcend the judgment of human laws. So, when these trees start sprouting everywhere within our society, producing the fruit that it's in their nature to bring forth, the result is a rising tide of righteousness that floats the nation. ("Righteousness exalts a nation..." Proverbs 14:34)

Now, the opening paragraph mentioned something of "roads intersecting in time and eternity." That wasn't poetic hyperbole either. Seriously, America stands at a threshold today, wondering what lies beyond. We're launching into a new year bewildered and fearful. Just in the last two years, we've been blindsided by a pandemic that's still raging, witnessed near-unprecedented political warfare, rioting and crime, and many have lost their jobs or have a vague premonition of imminent financial ruin in the months ahead. Not to mention ticking time bombs such as Iran and North Korea, which could conceivably reappear on the world stage and trigger a nasty armed conflict at any time.

In the midst of all this, we observe a renewed yearning in America's soul for righteousness. From the platforms of "social justice warriors," civil rights activists, paramilitary clubs of all persuasions—right, left, or sideways—and from the halls of congress down to the local bar stool, the national awareness has shifted dramatically to the plight of marginalized groups within our society, to laws that are "unjust" (whether in reality or perception), to the issues of poverty, homelessness, substance abuse, and ... you name it. What our nation craves, without knowing it, is **righteousness**.

What about the Church? Our knee-jerk reaction, more often than not, is to condemn these voices for justice, to avoid unpleasant conversations or gatherings, to retreat into our little safe spaces hoping the conflagration passes over us quickly so we can go back to minding our own business undisturbed.

But this is a prophetic moment! Church, let us not miss the window. Think of it: a new year, a new climate in our nation, people yearning for righteousness and willing to take action (misguided though it may often be) to make our country a better place. Why, we haven't seen such a perfect storm since the '60s!

"Prophetic" ... a curious word, though it really shouldn't be mysterious or spooky to us believers. In fact, I Samuel 9:9 breaks it down for us: "(Formerly in Israel, when a man went to inquire of God, he spoke thus: 'Come, let us go to the seer'; for he who is now called a prophet was formerly called a seer.)" So, a prophetic person is simply one who has God-given insight into—who **sees**—what God is doing. And, through the work of the Holy Spirit Who abides in us, we should all have a measure of "seeing," especially as it relates to our mission in this world.

Jesus rebuked the Pharisees and Sadducees in Matthew 16 because they failed to "discern the signs of the times." In contrast, the Sons of Issachar (which we already alluded to) in David's day were commended because they "understood the times and what they should do." For my part, I want to be a Son of Issachar. That means "awakening out of sleep" and "lifting up my (ostrich) head" out of the sand to see what's going on and ... most importantly ... to "see what the Father is doing," as Jesus said, so that I may be a part of it.

Let's consider Dr. Martin Luther King, Jr., whose birthday we observe this month. (Another intersection of time and eternity.) Dr. King is the only man to have a U.S. holiday named in his honor, who was not a U.S. president. At the age of 35, Dr. King was the youngest person ever to receive a Nobel Peace Prize. He may also have been the man who traveled the longest road to that prize—cussed out, abused, and arrested 29 times in his fight for righteousness, this modern-day prophet never quit because, as he said in his famous speech two days before his assassination, "We've got some difficult days ahead. But it doesn't matter with me now. Because I've been to the mountaintop.... And I've looked over. And I've seen the promised land. I may not get there with you. But I want you to know tonight, that we, as a people, will get to the promised land."

Dr. Martin Luther King, Jr. had his flaws. Every human vessel does. But he was fit for the Master's use because he had those three crucial qualities that made him a seed of righteousness: **life**, **character**, and **connection**. We know that he was tapped into Jesus, the source of true **life**, without Whom he could never have faced down the Goliaths of racial injustice and prevailed. But let's take a closer look at the other two qualities.

A seed of righteousness—which is to become a tree of righteousness—has its **character**, its life plan, imprinted into its DNA. Now, whether we realize it or not, each of us was conceived in the heart of our Creator and imprinted with His life plan before the human conception event took place. We just need to find out what that plan is ... or, at least, the first bread crumb He is pleased to reveal, which will start us down the path to finding the next bread crumb, then the next, until we attain that destiny.

Jesus, for example, being God Himself, knew precisely what

the plan was in full detail. Hence, we see Him at the age of twelve already "about His Father's business." Some believers may have a similar experience of realizing their life calling quite early on. Dr. King had such an experience, as we saw in the opening quote from his autobiography where he tells about riding the bus to high school. Not only did he have a deep passion for righteousness—in the area of racial justice, in this case—but he handled it in a prophetic way.

"I would end up having to go to the back of that bus with my body, but every time I got on that bus I left my mind up on the front seat. And I said to myself, 'One of these days, I'm going to put my body up there where my mind is.'"

In other words, when the young M.L. King boarded the school bus each day, he would envision his mind being planted on the very front seat of the bus. And he knew that one day the rest of him would follow ... which symbolized, from his adolescent perspective, the glorious achievement of racial justice for himself and his people. Wow! Now, he surely didn't have a clue as to how he would ultimately get to sit in that front seat, but he did have a passion and a vision. Oh, and one more thing: **connection**.

As the angel Clarence's character said in "It's a Wonderful Life," "One man's life touches so many others..." Just as a seed must interact with the soil, nutrients, heat, and ultimately sunlight and air, to become a fruit-bearing tree, we trees of righteousness require **connection**. We will never bear fruit in a vacuum.

Those connections may vary widely depending how God programmed us, but there must be connection nonetheless. For some of us, it's a church prayer group, social media outlets, or "networking" in our career. Dr. King not only learned to socialize and seek input from others at a young age (as his autobiography tells us), but he trained in public speaking during his high school years and planned to attend seminary.

"My call to the ministry was not a miraculous or supernatural something. On the contrary, it was an inner urge calling me to serve humanity." Dr. Martin Luther King, Jr. entered Crozer Seminary at the age of nineteen and graduated three years later. **Connection**. Without it, we are lifeless and fruitless.

What is the most productive way we can kick off this new year? Lift up our heads, seek to understand the times and what we should do, and learn more about saints gone before us who have fallen into the ground, died, and emerged as towering trees of righteousness, serving the purposes of God in their generation.

In conclusion, let's review a few well-known, inspirational quotes from Dr. Martin Luther King, Jr.

"We will not be satisfied until justice rolls down like waters."

"Communism will never be defeated by atomic bombs. Our greatest defense against Communism is to take offensive action on behalf of justice and righteousness. We must seek to remove conditions of poverty, injustice, and racial discrimination."

"Yes, if you want to say that I was a drum major, say that I was a drum major for justice. Say that I was a drum major for peace. I was a drum major for righteousness. And all of the other shallow things will not matter. I won't have any money to leave behind. I won't have the fine and luxurious things of life to leave behind. But I just want to leave a committed life behind. And that's all I want to say."

Why not pray ...

"Dear Father: Joining the ranks of those who mourn our fallen society, I truly want to make a difference. I look not to the past—years I've wasted, opportunities missed—but to the future. Thank You for being the ever-merciful and loving God of second, third, and infinite chances. But I don't want to miss the ones you send my way this year, this week ... ***today****. I can't go on comfortably isolating myself from Your flow of* ***life****, from the* ***character*** *and calling You've programmed into me, and from the* ***connections*** *I need with those You've placed in my life. Please heal my vision, fan the flames of my first love, and grow me into a tree bearing fruit of righteousness in abundance. I know I'm not Dr. King. But I also know that You have a unique part for me to play as I seek Your kingdom, Your righteousness. Plant my head on the front seat of the bus—whatever bus You've called me to board—and help me work tirelessly till the day when I see my whole body in that seat as well!*
In Jesus' name. Amen"

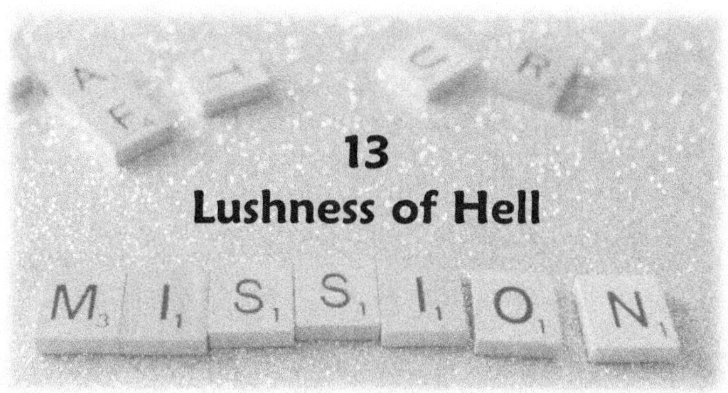

13
Lushness of Hell

"... The LORD has anointed Me ... To console those who mourn in Zion ... And they shall rebuild the old ruins, they shall raise up the former desolations, and they shall repair the ruined cities, the desolations of many generations." (Isaiah 61:1b-4)

The story is told about when Satan summoned the archdemon in charge of hell's wards and habitats to lead him on an impromptu inspection. Entering the gateway to the first region, the archdemon showed off the new, highly efficient inferno-thermal energy furnaces used to power the hot tubs of boiling oil where hapless souls were subjected to their daily bath.

In the next region, the devil was given a demonstration of the latest upgrade—maglev tracks where souls were fastened upside down by their ankles and whisked through a variety of automatic torture stations, where they were whipped, flayed, and flambéed in rapid succession.

And so it went. As the archdemon opened one massive gate after another and walked his master through the screaming hordes of tortured souls in each flaming ward, he received fresh plaudits for his fine work to improve the operations of hell.

Until they passed through another gate, where Satan was

astonished to find ... orchards laden with summer fruit, birds twittering in the branches, towering palm trees, fields of wheat and a gentle breeze pregnant with the scent of fresh alfalfa. The devil was beside himself. "What the heaven is going on here!?"

"Oh, Master, you know...!" the archdemon whimpered. *"It's just those dratted Jews and their irrigation projects!"*

On our own grand tour of the Isaiah 61 Messianic Age prophecy, we have been studying Christ's chosen few—the Blessed Mourners, we call them—whom He ordained and empowered to carry on His work on Earth. They have already been gloriously equipped in verse 3 with beauty, joy, praise, and towering righteousness, and the time has come at last for them to sally forth and, well ... do something! But, just *what* does our Lord have in mind for them to do?

"They shall rebuild the old ruins, they shall raise up the former desolations, and they shall repair the ruined cities, the desolations of many generations."

The language here could not be more precise, nor the picture painted, more vivid. We're not talking about a fresh coat of paint or patching up a leaky roof. No ... it's about **ruins. Desolation. Ruined cities.** Think of the once-proud city of Cologne after World War II. Then imagine that it had lain abandoned and utterly crumbling for yet another hundred years. Now it's 2045 and ... in marches the U.S. Army Corps of Engineers to help repair, raise up, and rebuild. *Talk about a daunting task!*

Back to our little story about lush orchards in hell. (And, hey... I happen to be of Jewish lineage, and we Jews do love to poke fun at ourselves! If you don't believe it, check out Dan Greenburg's 1960s bestseller, *How to Be a Jewish Mother.*) But our mid-century anecdote about hell is actually a nod to the awesome tenacity of Jewish immigrants, especially those pouring into Palestine after World War II, as they set out to reclaim vast swaths of the most dry, desolate land—what had been, three millennia earlier, known as the "land flowing with milk and honey." They faced a task nearly as daunting as did the Corps of Engineers in our Cologne analogy.

Now, there's nothing esoteric about Isaiah 61:4. These Blessed Mourners are quite clearly anointed with the Holy Spirit and power to repair and rebuild, to raise up a "city set on a hill" whose light beckons all who are weary, downtrodden, and oppressed by the devil to find our Savior's life in abundance. And raise it up they shall.

In fact, the ruins of that city are with us even now. It was a powerhouse of glory in the first century but, as the faith of many grew cold, it transfigured into the "desolation" we have today. Granted, there is plenty of life among the ruins, but nothing that holds a candle to the Early Church.

So ... just how do we go about rebuilding? In Jesus' day, crowds would follow Him out of town—into the hilly pastures or by the seaside boat launches—and listen to His words of life. Shall we plan "Jesus mega-rallies" at the nearest marina or cornfield? Or perhaps ... As recently as the 1950s and '60s, healing evangelists toured the country in circus tents, drawing in thousands to hear the gospel. So, maybe we resurrect the mid-century "Jesus tent tour" model, complete with sawdust on the ground and wooden folding chairs?

Isaiah 43:19 suggests otherwise. "See, I am doing a new thing! Now it springs up; do you not perceive it? I am making a way in the wilderness and streams in the wasteland." Our God is the same yesterday, today, and forever, and yet ... He is eternally full of surprises!

In the power of their Lord and Savior Jesus Christ, the Blessed Mourners, the spiritual sons and daughters of Abraham, **shall** embark on the greatest "irrigation project" of all time, bringing streams into the wasteland—abundant, vibrant life to the ruins of the Church in our generation. And it likely won't look anything like past revivals; it will be **something utterly new**.

Can this indeed happen right here in America? Nothing is impossible for God. Let's just give Him something to work with! A few Blessed Mourners who care enough to give their "utmost for His highest."

Why not pray ...

"Dear Father, as I ponder the "dry bones" of spiritual life in my generation ... they seem desperately dry. But reading Isaiah 61:4, there's a glimmer of hope! If I'm truly called to continue Jesus' ministry on Earth, I have to believe that these dry bones can live, that revival can come to America once again. And never have we needed it so! I don't know where to begin, but I'm willing. I want to be part of the solution, no longer part of the problem. Please, Lord, show me where to get started: this year, this month, this week! I'll be watching and listening for Your answer.
In Jesus' name. Amen"

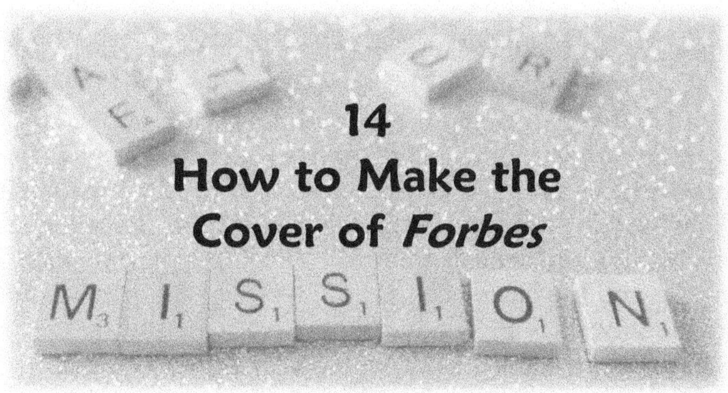

14
How to Make the Cover of *Forbes*

"... The LORD has anointed Me ... To console those who mourn in Zion ... Strangers shall stand and feed your flocks ..." (Isaiah 61:1b-5)

> According to [Strive] Masiyiwa, a devout Christian, prayers are essential for success in business.... Employees at Econet and people close to Masiyiwa confirm that the tycoon never takes any important business decision before first going on his knees. Judging by Econet's raving success, Masiyiwa's prayers actually work. Prayers may work for you as well.
>
> (*Forbes* Magazine, Feb. 24, 2013, excerpts)

Who is this Strive Masiyiwa, and what has he accomplished? Clearly something phenomenal, that the black-tie publication *Forbes* should feel compelled to broach the topic of prayer. (And *Forbes Africa* did a follow-up article a year later, in February 2014, with Masiyiwa's picture smack on the cover.)

To further quote the article:

"Today, Econet Wireless is an investor's delight. It is easily Zimbabwe's most successful corporation. It is Zimbabwe's largest mobile telecoms firm, with a subscriber base of over 6 million. Its profits for the year ended February 2011 stood at over $145 million and the Johannesburg-headquartered company has operations in Burundi, Lesotho, Kenya, Nigeria, Botswana and Rwanda. Econet has a market capitalization in the region of $600 million. Strive Masiyiwa, the unassuming and soft-spoken founder of the telecoms giant, is the richest person to emerge from Zimbabwe. You can glean important business and life lessons by taking a close look at what made Strive Masiyiwa a successful billionaire telecoms tycoon."

Besides Masiyiwa's success in business, he is known for his longtime friendship with the late Kofi Annan, Secretary-General of the United Nations, as well as his astounding philanthropic acts, such as feeding 40,000 orphans and providing educational scholarships to 250,000 youth in Africa.

But what's all this got to do with Isaiah 61, the "Messianic Playbook"?

Our journey so far through this glorious chapter has been something of a pleasure tour. It began with our Lord unfurling, in first person, His agenda to seek and save humanity. He then zooms in on the corps of Blessed Mourners—those who lament the lost state of their world and say, "Here am I, Lord, send me!"—and switches to third person, describing the magnificent way in which they will carry on His earthly work.

But then, verse 5 ... a jump scene! It's like you're drifting serenely along through Disneyland's iconic "It's a Small World" exhibit, when suddenly ... ***Wham!*** There's the T-Rex from Jurassic Park—*in your face*—with its curly, slimy tongue!

That's the effect when our Lord abruptly switches to second person, addressing **you**—"Strangers shall stand and feed **your** flocks"—and He continues in the second person right into verse 7. Why? Well, sure ... He wants to get our attention. But there's more to it than that. After all, God isn't all that into special movie effects.

While the preceding verses are a glorious narrative, to be continued midway through verse 7, this particular segment—verses 5 through 7a—is a divine blessing pronounced directly upon the reader. It's Christ Himself pouring the holy anointing oil of promise upon the blessed mourner's head as He utters these words of benediction.

Now, there are two conflicting schools of thought regarding success in life and business in the New Testament age. While those in one camp maintain that God wants all His children fat and happy, the opposing camp waves the tattered flag of the "holy indigent." So, which is right? Does God want us to prosper, or does He not? Did the blessings of the patriarchs come with a divine expiration date?

The fact is, we're asking the wrong question.

As the Apostle Paul explains at great lengths in his writings, the New Covenant ushered in by the Messiah of Isaiah 61 is superior to the Old Covenant in every way. Which means that our true question should be, "How will the Christian's material success **differ** from, and **exceed**, what was promised to the faithful of Israel?"

The answer is simple: "It's all about Jesus now."

And that's where both schools of prosperity thinking often miss the mark. Do the writers of *Forbes* Magazine gush with admiration when they see Christians parading their dazzling opulence? Or their pious poverty? *Neither, nohow!*

But show them a devout, humble, unassuming believer who also happens to be a business genius, rubbing shoulders with the likes of Kofi Annan, while feeding 40,000 orphans and educating 250,000 underprivileged youth—all powered by prayer? Well, *now* we have a story worth printing!

"Strangers shall stand and feed your flocks ..." Yes, we will have "flocks": in modern terms, "abundance of all we need in life, work, and business." And strangers—those who heretofore knew neither us nor the Lord we serve—will be drawn to us, just as God drew the animals to Noah's ark, to be instrumental in the support and furtherance of all the He's doing in our lives.

But this only happens when we put God first. When we come to the realization that all we possess in life is His. When we hold His blessings in an open hand, ready to give back to our Lord first, and also to those in need that He sends our way.

In Jesus' first major sermon, the one on the mount, He revealed the eternal principle of provision: that we need not fret and grasp for the things we need in life, but "seek first His kingdom and His righteousness," and then all we need will be given to us. **Given to us!** Yes, God does indeed want to give us everything we need. He has flocks to give—the cattle on a thousand hills. And it's **all ours** when we finally realize, deep down, that it's **all His.**

Why not pray ...

"Dear Father, thank you for raising up shining examples of true, humble, godly success, such as Strive Masiyiwa. Though I have no aspirations of being a multinational business tycoon, I want what he has—a life of prayer, generosity, humility ... and, yes, ***success****—so the "strangers" of the world will recognize the power of prayer and be drawn to Your light. Thank you for Your direct words of benediction in Isaiah 61:5. I'll take that!*
In Jesus' name. Amen"

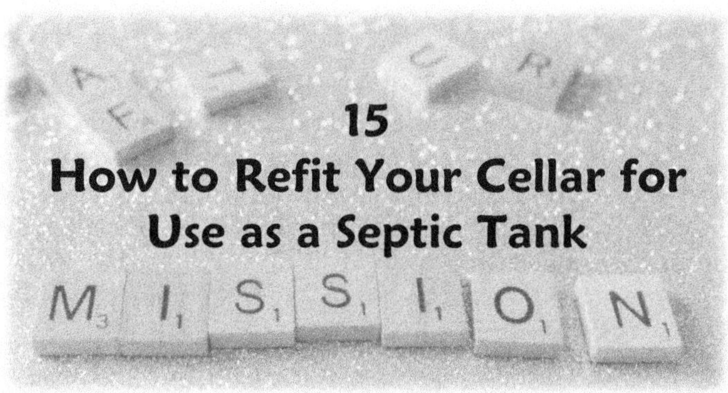

15
How to Refit Your Cellar for Use as a Septic Tank

"... The LORD has anointed Me ... To console those who mourn in Zion ... And the sons of the foreigner shall be your plowmen and your vinedressers." (Isaiah 61:1b-5b)

"Good morning, Eladio. Sorry to be a bearer of bad news, but ... ***We have a PROBLEM!!!!!"***

So began a miserable conversation with my building contractor, Eladio Stoltzfus. On a miserable day. That turned into a miserable month.

Located in rural Maryland, my home doesn't enjoy the convenience of being tied into a municipal sewer complex. Instead, we have the next-best alternative, which is a private, underground septic system. And, if you know anything about septics, they either work ... or they **don't**. And on this particular day? Suffice it to say that my brand-spanking new system definitely **didn't**!

All I ask of a septic system is, when I flush, I want things gone. Gone for **good—no returns, please**! But on this dismal morning, as I stepped down into my lovely, finished basement ... *Horrors!* Returns **everywhere**! Shooting out of the septic vent ... all across the floor!

Freeze scene ... (We'll be back!)

Continuing our tour of Isaiah 61, the Messianic Playbook, we come to this curious statement, this glorious promise made to the Blessed Mourners—that unique group we've been studying who profoundly lament the sinful, fallen state of their society, and who are ready to commit their lives to being ambassadors of change:
"... The sons of the foreigner [alien] shall be your plowmen and your vinedressers."

As with any piece of God-given Scripture, this one can be, and indeed has been, wrenched out of its rightful context by spokesmen—on both sides of the debate—of social policies ranging from slavery in the 18th and 19th centuries, to immigration reform in our own time.

But, to those of us who identify as heirs to the promises in Isaiah 61, the burning question is twofold: What was the statement's meaning to its original audience? And, what should it look like for us, living now in the Messianic Age?

We cannot arrive at the second answer without an accurate perspective on the first. When the Holy Spirit, through the prophet Isaiah, spoke of **foreigners**—or **"aliens,"** as the King James and other versions render it—He was **not** referring to the idolatrous, perverted people groups who had inhabited (and were still inhabiting, contrary to God's perfect will ... but that' a topic for another study!) the "promised land" of Canaan. Those cultures were so utterly corrupt, immersed in sexual immorality, infant sacrifice, and other abominable behavior that God's people were ordered to wipe them out. Make no treaties with them, no intermarriage, no working relationships. No "plowmen and vinedressers." Nada!
On the other hand, God called for quite a different sort of treatment for foreigners – aliens – who out of admiration for the people of God, the Israelites, chose to live among them. There were, in fact, countless such immigrants from the surrounding nations. The Lord was quite in favor of this state

of affairs. In fact, when we peek at the previous chapter, Isaiah 60, it says, "... The Lord will arise over you, and His glory will be seen upon you. The Gentiles shall come to your light, and kings to the brightness of your rising." (vv. 2b-3)

And provided these Gentiles honored God and observed the Law of Moses (see Leviticus 24:22), they were to be treated as equals and not oppressed or enslaved (Leviticus 19:33-34). On the contrary, foreigners would often move to Israel to be "plowmen and vinedressers" because they knew they could expect honest, godly employers—a much better situation than in their own lands.

But now, back to ... **How** does all of this relate to my heretofore-lovely basement awash in raw sewage?

Well, it has to do with the second part of our question regarding today's Isaiah 61 segment: What should this promise—"The sons of the foreigner [alien] shall be your plowmen and your vinedressers"—look like for **us**, living now in the Messianic Age?

If you're at all familiar with Pennsylvania Dutch names, you've probably guessed by now that Eladio Stoltzfus is a member of the Amish community. In fact, having lived right on the Pennsylvania border for the past 28 years, I've found it wise to engage the services of Amish-owned companies such as Eladio's whenever I need something done **right**. Fine Amish businessmen have replaced my roof, remodeled my kitchen, built the furniture for my home, provided tree service, excavation services, and constructed a very large addition on the back of my house.
Now, if you have any experience with home projects, you know that things don't always go as expected. And, that's where members of the Amish community shine, when it comes to a godly work ethic, pride in their craftsmanship, making things right when they go amiss, and honesty—"to a fault"!

In the sad case of my septic fiasco, it all began with the county's requirement that we move the existing septic tank further from the house before we could build the addition. So, my contractor "subbed" the work, in good faith, to another company (not Amish) who, as it turned out, didn't know a septic tank from a hole in their head. They properly crushed the old tank and trucked in a brand new one, dug the hole, and plopped it in ... but not deep enough. So, the line from the house to the tank was running *uphill*. And after a number of weeks, a symphony of factors including the viscosity of liquids and solids, and a pesky little force known as "gravity" ... resulted in a clogged sewage line and ... you know the rest of that story!

But the "miserable day that turned into a miserable month" could have been much, much worse. In short, the subcontractor did *not* rectify his mistake, even after we hired an independent inspector who confirmed that the root cause was the tank not being installed deep enough and the line running uphill. Instead, Eladio Stoltzfus himself paid **out of pocket** (over $3000) to hire another excavating company—**Amish, this time!**—to exhume the tank, dig the pit deeper, reinstall the tank, clear out and rerun the lines, and even replant the lawn that had been disturbed. He never once complained or tried to deflect blame.

And that was just one example of the numerous little issues—every construction project has them!—that Eladio dealt with in a manner that was more than just "professional"; it was always gracious and godly. In fact, ask anyone living near one of the many Amish communities across the U.S. who has had an opportunity to work with an Amish contractor, and you'll find that, more than likely, they would never take their work elsewhere.

As for "plowmen and vinedressers," I've found that Amish-owned companies don't just employ "their own"; they also hire skilled workers from all walks of life who seem thrilled to be working for an Amish firm. One of Eladio's employees, a master carpenter who spent weeks doing the interior finishing work on my house addition, confided that, during the twelve years he's worked for Eladio, he has been offered work by other (non-Amish) companies, often for a higher salary, but always turns it down. "I could never find someone who treats his employees with such honesty and respect," he said.

In retrospect, our previous study focused on Isaiah 61:5a, "Strangers shall stand and feed your flocks." We found that, not only does our Lord wish to bless us in work and business when we're faithful and put His kingdom first, but He also causes "strangers"—non-believers—to appreciate and support what we're doing.

To round it out, verse 5b, "... The sons of the foreigner [alien] shall be your plowmen and your vinedressers," echoes the glorious promises of Isaiah 60. (Read that entire chapter when you have a chance!) The last shall be first. The meek shall inherit the earth. The lowly, humble, god-fearing servant of God shall, in fact, be the head and not the tail! A city set on a hill. Gentiles shall come to our light, and kings to the brightness of our rising.

Why? Because we're brilliant and deserving of adulation? Not likely. Rather, it's because the Light in us is Jesus, and we're to draw all men to Him.

My friend, the master carpenter who works for Eladio Stoltzfus, is not a Christian ... yet. But he's keenly aware of the light he sees in his employer's spirit, and he's "almost persuaded" to be a Christian himself. Any day now! The Holy Spirit is still at work.

Why not pray ...

"Dear Father,
How unsearchable are Your judgments, and Your ways past finding out! (Romans 11:33) Thank you for promising to bless us, Your faithful servants, even in the apparently mundane dimension of work and business, so those who are alien to Your love and character will see them reflected in our own lives, want to partner with us, work with us or for us, and ultimately come to know the same God we serve.
In Jesus' name. Amen"

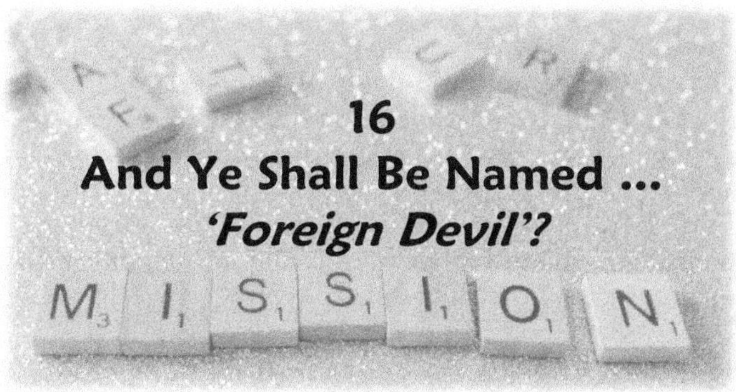

16
And Ye Shall Be Named ... *'Foreign Devil'?*

"... The LORD has anointed Me ... To console those who mourn in Zion ... But you shall be named the priests of the Lord." (Isaiah 61:1b-6a)

> Life is pitiful, death so familiar, suffering and pain so common, yet I would not be anywhere else. Do not wish me out of this or in any way seek to get me out, for I will not be got out while this trial is on. These are my people, God has given them to me, and I will live or die for Him and His glory.
>
> (Gladys Aylward, Missionary to China, during the Japanese Occupation)

Our latest stop along the glorious Isaiah 61 prophetic journey is this somewhat bewildering statement, made, of course, to the same Blessed Mourners we've been studying—those so utterly broken-hearted at the fallen state of their world, so outrageously sold out to Jesus, that they're ready to make a difference, whatever the cost:

"But you shall be named the priests of the Lord."

"But, Lord," we might say, "with all due respect ... You're obviously confused! Jesus Himself revealed the 61st chapter of Isaiah to be a New Testament prophecy when He said,

'Today this Scripture is fulfilled in your hearing.' (Luke 4:21) And, You know ... **not** every New Testament believer is a priest. In fact, Protestants believe that **no one** can be a priest anymore except Christ Himself—our final, eternal High Priest. (Hebrews 10:11-14)"

To which, our loving Father would remind us that the apostle Peter, inspired by the Holy Spirit, wrote:

"...You also, as living stones, are being built up a spiritual house, a **holy priesthood**..." (I Peter 2:5)

And he goes on to say:

"But you are a chosen generation, a **royal priesthood**, a holy nation, His own special people, that you may proclaim the praises of Him who called you out of darkness into His marvelous light;" (I Peter 2:9)

And, to whom was Peter addressing these statements? To a New Testament audience of believers, specifically defined as: elect by **God the Father**, sanctified by the **Holy Spirit**, and washed in the blood of **Jesus Christ**! (See I Peter 1:1-2)

Well, I guess if the Holy Trinity is in agreement that I'm a priest—a "royal" and "holy" one, no less!—that not only settles the matter, but ... *leapin' lizards!* ... I'd better hop to it and find out what's expected of me in this role!

It's quite simple, really. So simple, in fact, that we may have just now missed it. Back to I Peter 2:9: "But you are ... a **royal priesthood ... [so] that** you may proclaim the praises of Him who called you out of darkness into His marvelous light."

That's it!?

That's it, indeed. And yet, it's **huge**! To truly unpack the concept of being "His own special people ... proclaim[ing His] praises," would require opening the bottomless treasure chest of Isaiah 62—the glorious sequel to Isaiah 61 that continues the prophecy from the Messianic Age on into the Age to Come (i.e., upon Messiah's return). And, though that's outside the scope of this series, we can venture to crack open the lid of that chest and steal a peek:

"You who make mention of the Lord, do not keep silent, and give Him no rest till He establishes and till He makes Jerusalem a praise in the earth." (Isaiah 62:6b-7)

So, what does a chosen, royal, holy, special, **New Testament** generation of priests look like? Same idea as the Old Testament priesthood, but ever-so-much-more-so!

Under the Old Covenant, priests were God's representatives to inspire and instruct the people, administer judgment in righteousness, and accept the blood sacrifices on God's behalf to atone for sin. In short, their purpose in life was to "channel" (as best they could, given their flawed human nature) the character of God—Who is the Source of all inspiration, instruction, righteousness, and atonement.

So, what about a New Covenant priesthood? And **what** does Gladys Aylward have to do with all of this?

Gladys Aylward (1902-1970) was an ordinary English girl from a working-class family. She had to cut short her education at age 14 and go to work. At age 28, feeling God's call on her life to be a missionary to China, she attended Bible school for three months with China Inland Mission, but was told flat-out that she did not qualify for an assignment in China.

Not to be so easily dissuaded, Gladys took a job as a domestic helper (maid) in London and saved her shillings until she was able to purchase a railway ticket to the remote town of

Yangcheng, China where, she had been told, a lone elderly Englishwoman, Mrs. Jeannie Lawson, was serving as a missionary. The journey was fearfully difficult. At one point, Gladys was forced off the train by Russian soldiers, and she had to walk about thirty miles through the snow to the nearest village.

But when she arrived in Yangcheng, her difficulties began in earnest. In the midst of working long hours to rehabilitate a derelict old building into an inn for transient mule trains, and while struggling to learn the language and ways of a people who knew absolutely nothing of Judeo-Christian culture and niceties—where even the children looked on her as a "foreign devil" and would hurl dirt clods at her in the streets ... In the midst of all this, Gladys's missionary partner, Jeannie Lawson, fell from the second floor of the building they were restoring ... *and died!*

Now Gladys Aylward was all alone in a land that was not hers, surrounded by people who, for the most part, still did not understand nor appreciate what she was doing there, and with the China Inland Mission's assessment still heavy on her mind: "You're not qualified." **Now** was her opportunity to call it all a big mistake and make her way back home to England. And no one would have blamed her for doing so!

But Gladys understood one glorious concept that carried her through: that if God had called her to China—as she was utterly sure He had—then **this**, not England, was her home. And if God had called her to be a missionary, then that's precisely what she would be. Failure was impossible as long as God was behind her. In her own words:

"If God has called you to China or any other place and you are sure in your own heart, let nothing deter you. Remember, it is God who has called you and it is the same as when He called Moses or Samuel."

Fast-forward six years. Gladys Aylward, now a Chinese

citizen and the only white woman in Yangcheng, is running the missionary outpost known as "The Inn of the Eight Happinesses," preaching the gospel to travelers. She has adopted numerous Chinese children, whom she cares for at the mission. And, in her spare time, she travels the surrounding countryside as a government emissary to educate women about the new regulations against foot-binding ... and, of course, to share the good news of Jesus Christ wherever she goes.

By this time, the people who, in years past, had called her a "foreign devil" now referred to Gladys by a new and affectionate title: "Ai-weh-deh"—"The Virtuous One." See, she had earned the respect and love of everyone, from the children who once threw dirt clods at her, to the Mandarin official (what we would call a mayor) of Yangcheng, who considered her his "right-hand man." Gladys stood for righteousness and against oppression, often risking her life in the process, such as when she stepped into the local prison to intervene and defuse a violent prison riot in progress and to advocate for the prisoners' welfare with the Yangcheng leadership.

Gladys Aylward's capping achievement was in 1938, when the Japanese violence reached her beloved Yangcheng, and she found herself leading 100 children to safety through a perilous war zone. But in her own words, again:

"Life is pitiful, death so familiar, suffering and pain so common, yet I would not be anywhere else. Do not wish me out of this or in any way seek to get me out, for I will not be got out while this trial is on. These are my people, God has given them to me, and I will live or die for Him and His glory."

In conclusion, we see a passionately brave hero of the faith whose life was a monument of "praise in the earth"—to inspiration, instruction, righteousness, and the glorious gospel of redemption in Jesus Christ.

But, wait! Isn't that the definition of a New Testament **priest**? Indeed it is, hallelujah! And where could we find a better example than Gladys Aylward?

And now, as Christ Himself would say, "Go and do thou likewise!"

To find out more about this remarkable lady, read her autobiography, *Gladys Aylward: The Little Woman* (1970). Or, for a synoptic view (if more than a bit Hollywoodized), watch the movie *The Inn of the Sixth Happiness* (1958).

Why not pray ...

"Dear Father,
I've never thought of myself as a "holy, royal priest." But, at Your word, so be it! Please, may I never rest—nor give You rest—until You've birthed Your own high-priestly heart within me. Please do ***in*** *me all you* ***need*** *to ... so You can do* ***through*** *me all You* ***want*** *to!*
In Jesus' name. Amen"

17
Dost Covet Destruction, Thou Maniac?

"... The LORD has anointed Me ... To console those who mourn in Zion ... They shall call you the Servants of our God." (Isaiah 61:1b-6b)

> In the midst of the talk I let drop a complimentary word about King Arthur, forgetting for the moment how this woman [Queen Morgan le Fay] hated her brother. That one little compliment was enough. She clouded up like storm; she called for her guards, and said, "Hale me these varlets to the dungeons."
>
> That struck cold on my ears, for her dungeons had a reputation. Nothing occurred to me to say or do. But not so with [my companion] Sandy. As the guard laid a hand upon me, she piped up with the tranquilest confidence, and said, "...Dost covet destruction, thou maniac!? It is *The Boss!*"
>
> The effect upon madame was electrical. It cleared her countenance and brought back her smiles and all her persuasive graces and blandishments.... She said, "I did but play this little jest with hope to surprise you into some display of your art, as not doubting you would blast the guards with occult fires, consuming them to ashes on the spot, a marvel much beyond mine own ability, yet one which I have long been childishly curious to see."

The guards were less curious, and got out as soon as they got permission.

* * *

[Later, in the queen's dungeon:]
"Ye will do in all things as this lord shall command," [said Morgan le Fay]. "It is *The Boss....*"

The queen's guards fell into line, and she and they marched away, with their torch-bearers, and woke the echoes of the cavernous tunnels with the measured beat of their retreating footfalls. I had the prisoner taken from the rack and placed upon his bed, and medicaments applied to his hurts, and wine given him to drink....

Then I said, "Now, my friend, tell me your side of this matter ... If my reputation has come to you right and straight, you should not be afraid to speak."

[His wife] broke in, eagerly: "Ah, dear my lord, an ye will but persuade him! Consider how these his tortures wound me! Oh, and he will not speak! Whereas, the healing, the solace that lie in a blessed swift death ..."

"What are you maundering about? He's going out from here a free man and whole—he's not going to die."

The man's white face lit up, and the woman flung herself at me in a most surprising explosion of joy, and cried out: "He is saved!—for it is the king's word by the mouth of the king's servant—Arthur, the king whose word is gold!"

(From *A Connecticut Yankee In King Arthur's Court*, Chapters XVI and XVII [1889] Mark Twain, excerpts)

Our last Isaiah 61 expedition broke off mid-sentence, as we meditated on a solemn promise made to our Lord's Blessed Mourners (those who share His heart of compassion and action for the lost): "You shall be called priests of the Lord...." (verse 6a). And we discovered the blessed role of the believer as a New Testament priest: for inspiration, instruction, righteousness, and spreading the glorious gospel of redemption in Jesus Christ.

But then, verse 6b caps off that thought with the assurance that we will further be called "the Servants of our God."

OK, so the "priest" part sounded pretty good; but how does "servant" add anything?

"Servant of God": cliché, and pretext nowadays for anything from ... why the pastor doesn't need a raise, to ... why it's my "holy calling" to pontificate on social media. And yet, we know that Scripture contains no idle thought, so let's have a closer look at what this promise means: "**They shall call you** the Servants of our God."

Think of it! We who identify as Blessed Mourners are ordained by Jesus Christ Himself to carry on His Isaiah 61 commission until the end of the age. And we've already seen what-all that entails! In short, just like the Early Church, we're sent forth to turn the world upside down.

But how? Maybe you feel just as Moses did, as he expressed at the burning bush: (a) I'm not impressive, (b) I'm not good at public speaking, and (c) in the end ... why should anyone listen to me!?

Notice that God never disagreed with Moses' statements. Instead, he graciously helped Moses understand that it wasn't about him; it was about **Him**.

"God said to Moses, "I AM Who I AM." And He said, "Say this to the people of Israel, 'I AM has sent me to you.'" (Exodus 3:14) And, sure enough, the people responded by acknowledging him as a "Servant of our God." (Exodus 14:31) But it didn't stop there. Now that Moses was no longer just Moses, but a Servant of the Living "I AM" God ... he could stand before a king and **tell him what to do**: "Let My people go!"

Back to us ...
"But you shall be named the priests of the Lord." (Isaiah 61:6a) That's a fantastic start. But, as with Moses ... what are the chances that anyone will listen to us because we're priests? Not hardly! Which is why we need the rest of the sentence: "**They shall call you** the Servants of our God" (verse 6b).

When the World comes to realize—by witness of the Holy Spirit anointing upon us with revival and signs following (which are sadly a rare thing in the Church today, and for which we ought to be praying with every cell of our being ... but that's a topic for a different time)—that we are indeed representatives of Almighty God, **now** we too can stand before kings, principalities and powers, and **tell them what to do.**

Why? Because they can see and know that we are servants of a **higher** King. While verse 6a speaks to who **we** are, 6b is all about Who **He** is, in—and through—us.

In Mark Twain's novel *A Connecticut Yankee in King Arthur's Court*, we find the main character—a contemporary factory worker named Hank—transported magically back to sixth-century England where he becomes a servant and right-hand man to the fabulous King Arthur himself.

As "The Boss"—an honorary title of nobility that the people

had given him—Hank is able to walk into the castle of the wicked queenlet Morgan le Fay (who happens to be Arthur's sister) in a small neighboring kingdom and **tell her what to do**, including, in the end, emptying her dungeon of all its oppressed and tortured occupants. Why? Not because he was Hank Morgan, but by virtue of his rank as The Boss, servant of King Arthur—"the king whose word is gold!"

Sure, this stuff plays well in fiction. But in the real world? No way!

WAY!...

We already saw how the Israelites recognized Moses as a Servant of God, and he was able to stand before Pharaoh. Here are a few more historical examples of those who stood before kings:

- "Then Nebuchadnezzar came near to the door of the furnace of blazing fire; he responded and said, 'Shadrach, Meshach and Abed-nego, come out, you **servants of the most high God**, and come here!' Then Shadrach, Meshach and Abed-nego came out of the midst of the fire." (Daniel 3:26) These three were actually servants of Nebuchadnezzar, but he now realized that they were truly servants of a Higher Power. And he immediately issued a decree saying that anyone who should speak a word against the God of Shadrach, Meshach, and Abednego would do so at the peril of his life.
- "Then the king [Darius] arose very early in the morning and went in haste to the den of lions. And when he came to the den, he cried out with a lamenting voice to Daniel. The king spoke, saying to Daniel, 'Daniel, **servant of the living God**, has your God, whom you serve continually, been able to deliver you from the lions?'" (Daniel 6:19-

20) Though Daniel was in the service of Darius, now Darius recognized Who Daniel's **true** Master was. And he, too, immediately issued a decree: that all men, everywhere, should "tremble in fear" at the God of Daniel.

- Later, when Zerubbabel and the Jews began rebuilding the temple in Jerusalem, Tatnai, the governor of Palestine wrote a letter of complaint to Darius, saying, "Thus [Zerubbabel and his men] answered us, saying, 'We are the **servants of the God of heaven and earth** and are rebuilding the temple that was built many years ago, which a great king of Israel built and finished....'" (Ezra 5:11) On receipt of the letter, Darius not only dissed Governor Tatnai's complaint, but he validated Zerubbabel's title and claims, instructing the governor to actually fund the temple construction and not interfere with it under penalty of death.

But there's more ...

Not only does the Master give His servants grace to stand before a lost world, with its authorities and powers that be, and see His will be done because they realize we are His servants. He further gives us authority to successfully stand against spiritual principalities, powers, rulers of the darkness of this world, and spiritual wickedness in high places. (Ephesians 6:11-12)

Christ Himself affirmed this in Luke 10:17-19: "And the seventy returned again with joy, saying, 'Lord, even the devils are subject unto us through Thy name.' And He said unto them, 'I beheld Satan as lightning fall from heaven. Behold, I give unto you power to tread on serpents and scorpions, and over all the power of the enemy: and nothing shall by any means hurt you.'"

Why not pray ...

"Dear Father,
Thank you for ordaining me as a member of Your royal priesthood of believers to bring inspiration, instruction, righteousness, and spreading the glorious gospel of redemption in Jesus Christ. And yet, I have ***no*** *illusions of being able to accomplish this great task on my own. Birth in me a heart of prayer for sovereign revival—and may it begin with me through daily repentance—until Your power, anointing, and signs follow the Church in America once again. May we become that city on a hill, so men and women everywhere declare us to be* ***servants of God*** *... and come to our Master's light!*
In Jesus' name. Amen."

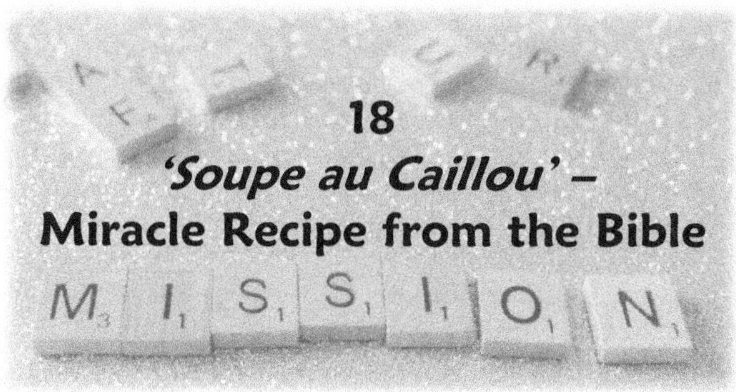

18
'Soupe au Caillou' – Miracle Recipe from the Bible

"... The LORD has anointed Me ... To console those who mourn in Zion ... You shall eat the riches of the Gentiles, and in their glory you shall boast." (Isaiah 61:1b-6c)

> Two travelers, dying of thirst and hunger, entered a farm and asked for something to fortify their feeble stomachs.
>
> "Gentlemen," said the farmer, "...leave! For we have neither meat nor bread."
>
> So begins the earliest known account, circa 1716, of the story "La Soupe au Caillou (Stone Soup)," by Anne-Marguerite Petit du Noyer (1663-1719), a.k.a. Madame Desnoyers.

Today's Isaiah 61 episode—following the story of Christ's dyed-in-the-wool, turn-the-world-upside-down brigade—brings us to a veritable meat-and-potatoes question: "How do these Blessed Mourners eat!?" Indeed, those of us who would answer this passage's high calling cannot but ask ourselves whether it includes "holy" hunger and ruination.

It's a fair question, and one that Peter himself raised in Mark 10. To which, our gracious Lord responded, "... There is no one who has left house or brothers or sisters or father or mother or wife or children or lands, for My sake and the gospel's, who shall not receive a hundredfold now in this time—houses and brothers and sisters and mothers and children and lands, with persecutions—and in the age to come, eternal life."

Or, for the flat-out meat-and-potatoes perspective, we have Matthew 6 (paraphrase mine): "Don't worry what you'll eat, drink, or wear. While the world is obsessing over those things, your Father's got you covered. Be a faithful Kingdom servant, and you'll see that His provision is automatic!"

While this sounds good on paper ... let's face it ... Jesus was just waxing poetic, right? And if we go to the original Greek, we'll discover that it works out to be, like, some abstruse spooky-spiritual meaning, right?

Wrong. Actually, the original Greek is equally clear and simple: "Don't worry, saying, 'What shall we eat/drink/wear?' Your Heavenly Father knows that you need these things. Seek first His Kingdom ..."

If you're starting to see a theme emerging here ... you're right!

- Mark 10: Seek to follow Christ over family and possessions: receive a hundredfold.
- Matthew 6: Seek His Kingdom over food/drink/clothing: receive all those things.

And our Isaiah 61 passage further connects the dots by saying, "You shall eat the riches of the Gentiles." Which, in today's New Testament context, equates to: "The Christian's provision will come at the hand of non-believers."

How so?

Think about it. Whatever your perceived source of income—whether a job, business, investments, Social Security (which is just another type of investment)—it all involves a transfer of "riches" from non-believers to you.

But here's where we get tripped up, especially when you add to the mix wars, health crises, economic downturns, investments "underwater" and what not. How am I to keep afloat when the buying power from my salary/business/investment/Social Security source is down, and the cost of living is through the clouds? What am I to eat, drink, and wear?

A Christian businessman friend called me just the other day. "What's your opinion on the coming recession?" he said. "It's not affected my business yet, but I have other friends that say theirs are slowing down significantly. And I'm getting worried."

It was an opportunity for me to share how the Lord had been changing my own perspective on this very topic. The bottom line is that the Christian's perceived sources of income are not **sources** at all; they're just **channels**. Our Heavenly Father—the One Who already knows what we need (Matthew 6)—**He** is the Source! As long as I consider my job and my business (I have both) as my sources, they will let me down. But when I trust the Lord as my Source, and I focus first on serving Him, then He takes care of dredging the channel when it's slow ... or changing channels if necessary. Economic drought cannot touch me so long as my trust is in Him.

"Blessed is the man who trusts in the Lord, and whose hope is the Lord. For he shall be like a tree planted by the waters, which spreads out its roots by the river, and will not fear when heat comes; but its leaf will be green, and will not be anxious in the year of drought, nor will cease from yielding fruit." (Jeremiah 17:7-8)

How does this jibe with the promise that we'll "eat the riches of the Gentiles"?

Our "Stone Soup" fable begins with two itinerant men desperately in need of a meal. The farmer and his neighbors have a rich supply of edibles to which these travelers at first seem to feel they are entitled simply by virtue of their hunger. But the farmer rebuffs them, saying deceitfully, "Leave! For we have neither meat nor bread."

However, when the protagonists change their approach to one of service, offering to fill a cauldron with lovely "stone soup" for the enjoyment of all ... suddenly, the "Gentiles" are happy to contribute of their riches—a cabbage here, some turnips, seasonings, a cut of meat, and so on. In the end, the travelers partook of a feast, though they'd added nothing but stones from the dusty road they traveled ... and a willingness to bless.

Why not pray ...

"Dear Father,
Thank You for Your compassionate foreknowledge of all I require for life and godliness—even the mundane necessities such as food and clothing. This world is not my home; but, as I'm passing through, develop in me the heart of a Kingdom servant. And may I come to understand, deep down, that You are the infinite Source of provision—not my job, business, or investments, but You alone. May I trust wholeheartedly in You and eat the riches of the "Gentiles" that You channel my way.
In Jesus' name. Amen."

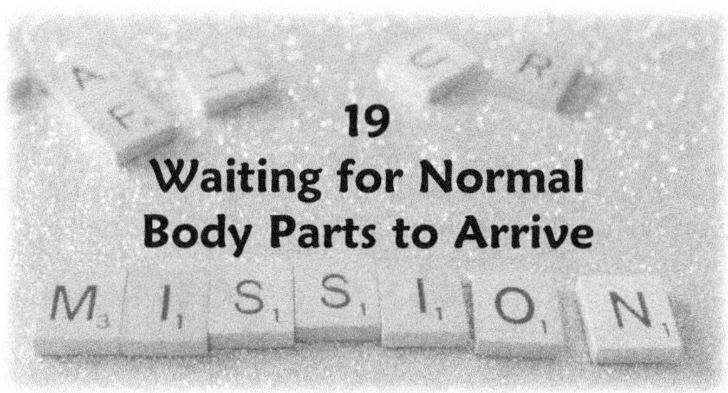

19
Waiting for Normal Body Parts to Arrive

"... The LORD has anointed Me ... To console those who mourn in Zion ... Instead of your shame you shall have double honor ..." (Isaiah 61:1b-7a)

> "I can't be a princess! I'm still waiting for normal body parts to arrive!"
>
> (Mia Thermopolis, from *The Princess Diaries* [2001] Walt Disney Pictures)

Today's portion of the magnificent Isaiah 61 treasure—the bequest of our Lord's Blessed Mourners—is in fact just a single facet of the multi-faced gem that is verse seven, which could itself spawn a thousand sermons. So, it is essential that we first look at the gem from all sides, then rightly divide it for the purposes of this study.

"Instead of your shame you shall have double honor, and instead of confusion they shall rejoice in their portion. Therefore in their land they shall possess double; everlasting joy shall be theirs." (Isaiah 61:7)

Wow! To begin with, we have three prominent themes: **honor** instead of shame; **possession** instead of confusion; and finally, the outcome—boundless, everlasting JOY. This devotional will focus on the first theme, **honor**.

But what's up with that pesky word "double"? Double honor. Double portion. Is it like when Mom and Dad would heap my plate with brussels sprouts and not let me exit the table till I'd finished every last one?

Thankfully, our Lord afflicts us neither with unmanageable "double portions" nor unsolvable riddles. In fact, Isaiah's 8th-century B.C. audience wouldn't even have done a double take. They were familiar with Old Testament law, wherein the "right of the firstborn" was a double portion of the inheritance (Deuteronomy 21:17), not to mention the double honor of continuing the family's patriarchal lineage (Genesis 49:3). So, while the words "portion," "land," and "possess" all speak of inheritance, the word "double" specifically focuses on **firstborn** inheritance.

OK, so what's a verse about firstborn inheritance doing *right smack in the middle*, literally, of God's promises to His Blessed Mourners (verses 3-11)?

Because it is absolutely **pivotal**! Think of the ground we've covered since verse 3. He first gives them "beauty for ashes": His eternal destiny in exchange for the ashes of their broken dreams. Right up through verse 6, where they "eat the riches of the Gentiles": His unlimited provision in exchange for the petty possessions and prestige they left behind.

Why? Because, as Paul said, "You died, and your life is hidden with Christ in God." (Colossians 3:3) Christ—Who is the image of the invisible God, the **Firstborn** of all creation. (Colossians 1:15) He is also head of the body, the church; and He is the beginning, the **Firstborn** from the dead (v. 18), and the **Firstborn** among many brethren. (Romans 8:29)

But it gets better....

Jesus Christ is indeed the firstborn among many brethren, since we are all sons of God through adoption. Thinking back to the Old Testament "right of the firstborn," that means Jesus gets a double portion of honor and inheritance, while we get ... the scraps, right?

No, no, NO, hallelujah! And herein lies the mystery of it all: that, having died, and now alive again "hidden with Christ in God," **we are all firstborn ... in Him!** Hebrews 12:22 speaks of the saints gone to be with Him as "the general assembly and church of the firstborn who are enrolled in heaven." And Romans 8:16b-17 speaks directly in terms of our inheritance: "...We are children of God. And if children, then heirs—heirs of God and **joint heirs** with Christ."

Let that sink in: **"joint heirs."** It's not a matter of Jesus, the Firstborn, getting a "double portion" and the rest of us getting what's left over. Rather, **in Him**, we are the church of the firstborn, joint-heirs with the one-and-only Firstborn, Jesus Christ. **In Him**, we enjoy that "double portion"—instead of shame, the firstborn's honor; and instead of confusion, the firstborn's possession. There are no leftovers. It's just the full firstborn's portion: **all things** for life and godliness.

Charles Spurgeon articulated this very truth quite eloquently in his impassioned sermon "The Joint Heirs and Their Divine Portion," delivered July 28, 1861:

> "And O my soul, thy portion cannot be slender nor thy dowry narrow, since it is the same inheritance which Christ has from His Father's hands. Weigh the riches of Christ in scales and his treasures in balances, and then think to count the treasures which belong to the saints. Reach the bottom of Christ's sea of joy, and then hope to understand the bliss which God hath prepared for them that love Him. Overleap the boundaries of Christ's possession if you can, and then dream of finding a limit to the possessions of the elect

> of God. 'All things are yours, for ye are Christ's and Christ is God's.' [Romans 8:17]"

Now, having surveyed the full breadth of verse 7, let's bite off, at last, today's theme: **honor** instead of shame. As joint heirs with Christ, one thing we receive is "double honor," that is, the **honor** of the firstborn Son. And yet, it's paradoxical because we enjoy that glorious honor only by giving it to Him, Who is the One and only Being entitled to it. As Paul stated, "May I never boast except in the cross of our Lord Jesus Christ, through which the world has been crucified to me, and I to the world." (Galatians 6:14) Meaning, my boast—my honor—lies in the fact that He is everything. I am nothing, and yet at the same time, I am everything **in Him**.

And, if I inherit all the honor of the Firstborn of God, there remains no place for shame. Why? Because, on the cross of our Lord Jesus Christ, He bore the utmost shame—**my** shame—so I no longer have to!

In our opening teaser, we recall Mia's shock on learning that she was heir to a kingdom she'd never even heard of: "I can't be a princess! I'm still waiting for normal body parts to arrive!"

In Disney's 2001 classic *The Princess Diaries*, Amelia "Mia" Thermopolis is ashamed of her looks, bullied by classmates, terrified to speak in front of class ... yeah, a typical fifteen-year-old. But when her world is turned upside down by the sudden revelation that she is a born princess, and soon to be queen, well ... watch the movie. But the point is that her surprise inheritance lifts her from shame to honor, from being a nobody to the place of preeminence among her people—a vantage point from which she can truly make a difference.

Why not pray ...

"Dear Father,
Thank You that I am part of that "chosen generation," that ***all things*** *are mine in Jesus Christ the Firstborn. From this place of strength, may I live—no longer I, but Christ in me—to reflect all honor and praise back to Him, that the world may come to His magnificent light!*
In Jesus' name. Amen."

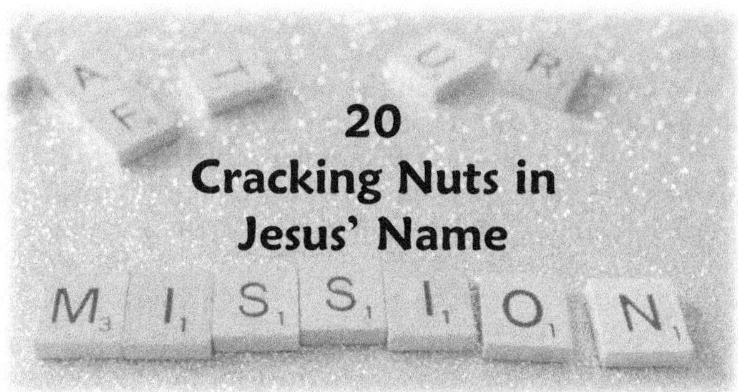

20
Cracking Nuts in Jesus' Name

"... The LORD has anointed Me ... To console those who mourn in Zion ... And instead of confusion they shall rejoice in their portion. Therefore in their land they shall possess double ..." (Isaiah 61:1b-7b)

> "Speak up, good lad, and fear nothing," said the King. "How used you the Great Seal of England?"
>
> Tom stammered a moment, in a pathetic confusion, then got it out—
>
> "To crack nuts with!"
>
> (From *The Prince and the Pauper*, Chapter XXXII [1881] Mark Twain)

On our fair ocean voyage through the Messianic 61st chapter of Isaiah, we found ourselves last time at a primary port of call: verse 7, which happens to be the midway point of the nine verses (3-11) that enumerate His promises to the Blessed Mourners—we who are to carry on our Lord's work till He returns.

And, as we noted, this most precious verse brings to light the nature of our inheritance in Jesus Christ, the Firstborn, Who is Himself the Heir of all things (Psalms 2:7-8). And what may that nature be? Simply put, that we ourselves become firstborn and inherit as such the firstborn's "double portion"—because we're **in Him**. That's right, **all** things for life and godliness. And the verse breaks it down further into three categories of inheritance: honor (which we already explored), possession, and joy. Let's talk about possession....

"... In their portion.... in their land," it says, "they shall possess double." (verse 7b) But what "land" are we talking about?

Under the Old Covenant, God has much to say about land—the land promised to Abraham and his descendants, which promise was fulfilled in the days of Joshua. Having brought His people out of Egypt (symbolic of Sin), through the Red Sea (which stood for salvation and baptism), Almighty God settled them in the "Promised Land," where they were to possess whatever the sole of their feet laid claim to (Joshua 1:3-6).

And, make no mistake, God's gifts and callings are irrevocable (Romans 11:29). He didn't feed His promises through some sort of giant shredder when Jesus arrived on the scene. In fact, the **only** thing He did shred was the veil that kept sinful man out of the Holy of Holies (Matthew 27:51), hallelujah! As for the **people** of Israel, they still figure in His end-time plan. (Read Romans chapter 11.) As does the **land** of Israel. (Read The Book of Revelation.)

But now that we've got all that straight ... Isaiah 61 is indisputably a New Covenant prophecy. We have that from the mouth of Christ Himself (Luke 4:21). Which means it has New Covenant meaning. **Including** the concept of **land**.

Having brought us out of Egypt (Sin), through the Red Sea of His precious blood, we now enter His promised land of **rest**. In fact, Father God devotes an entire chapter of the New Testament—Hebrews 4—to explaining the promised **land** we now enter, as being His place of **rest**. And Christ Himself used the analogy of **rest** in Matthew 11:28-30, where He speaks of entering a **yoke** with Him (meaning, we have work to do!) and finding it easy, light, and restful.

What does it all mean?

"As the Father has sent Me, I also send you." (John 20:21) We keep coming back to that thought in our study of Isaiah 61 because we know that Jesus read the passage, set its fulfillment in motion, and then commissioned **us**—His Blessed Mourners—to continue its fulfillment until the end of the age.

But, though the task seems daunting, it is easy, light, and restful when we are **in Him** —in His yoke. It is our inheritance, our possession, the Kingdom of God, our Great Commission, our life's labor in the fields of His harvest ... His **land**. His **rest**. Because He is carrying out that commission through us, IN US, as we are **in Him**, acting **in His name**.

In the words of the old song: *"When we stand in the name of Jesus / Tell me who can stand before us. / When we stand in the name of Jesus / We have the victory,"*

Which brings us to that giant in the world of literature, Mark Twain. When Twain published his first great work of historical fiction, *The Prince and the Pauper*, little did he know what a striking allegory it was to God's glorious New Covenant of grace.

In this masterpiece of a novel, we see the nine-year-old prince of Wales—soon to become King Edward VI—leaving his royal palace to take on the form of a pauper dressed in rags, sharing the sufferings of the common people (his subjects), who in turn mocked him and refused to believe he was their prince. And, by doing this, the prince enabled the *true* pauper boy, Tom Canty of Offal Court, to be clothed in his princely garments, inhabit his princely apartments, and even issue princely decrees—such as promoting a particularly loyal friend from earl to duke. Tom could do all of this because, when the prince **became** Tom, the *real* Tom, though born a pauper, **became** the prince and could act in his name.

And yet—*wonder of wonders!*—the punch line of Twain's story was the very thing our Lord would have us focus on today. When the true prince left Tom behind to act on his behalf, he left in his possession the most powerful weapon in the kingdom: the Great Seal of England. It had the power to enforce the king's law, to execute judgment on an enemy, to do wondrous things.

But poor Tom had no idea how to use the Great Seal. In fact, he didn't even know it *was* the Great Seal. What he did know, as we saw in our lead-in excerpt from the story, was that it functioned quite splendidly for cracking nuts!

O Blessed Mourner, think of it! Through the precious blood of Christ, we are privileged to have entered the promised land of rest **in Him,** beyond the veil, seated in the heavenly places of His firstborn inheritance, while living out His commission here on Earth, ambassadors of Heaven by His power and the authority of His Great Seal—His **name**. We have power to tread on spiritual serpents and scorpions, on all the powers of the enemy in the name of Jesus. To make a **difference**.

And yet, how often do we utter the mighty name of Jesus in prayer for ... cracking nuts? Prayers for ourselves only—our needs, our comforts?

Why not pray ...

"Dear Father,
When I stand before You on that day, and You ask, 'How did you use the Great Seal of Heaven?' may my reply not be, 'To crack nuts with!' Instead, I ask, place Your yoke upon me and

teach me. Together, may we work the fields of Your harvest, acting in the power of Jesus the Firstborn, speaking healing, deliverance, and salvation in Your name to all who are oppressed by the devil. Fulfilling the Isaiah 61 mandate. In Jesus' name. Amen."

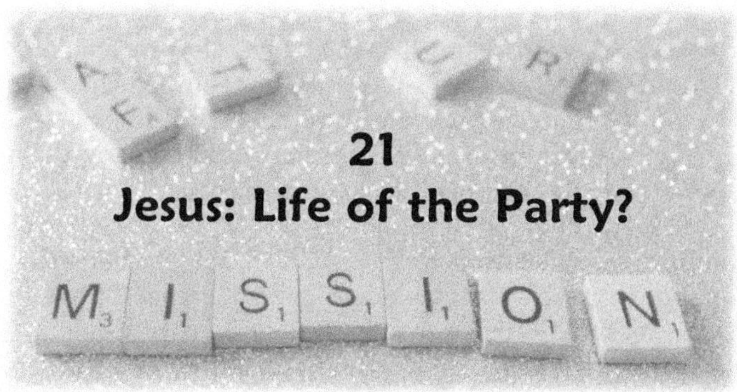

21
Jesus: Life of the Party?

"... The LORD has anointed Me ... To console those who mourn in Zion ... Therefore in their land they shall possess double; everlasting joy shall be theirs." (Isaiah 61:1b-7c)

> "...If God took the trouble to tell us eight hundred times to be glad and rejoice, He must want us to do it—*SOME!*
>
> (From *Pollyanna*, Chapter XXII [1913] Eleanor H. Porter)

When Eleanor Porter, an unassuming writer from Massachusetts in her early 40s, wrote the novel *Pollyanna*, little could she have imagined how it would "go viral." According to book publisher Simon & Schuster: "First published in 1913, her story spawned the formation of 'Glad' clubs all over the country, devoted to playing Pollyanna's famous game. *Pollyanna* has since sold over one million copies, been translated into several languages, and has become both a Broadway play and a Disney motion picture."

This might seem puzzling, since the term "Pollyanna" has, in our day, become synonymous with a certain detachment from reality, a tendency to pretend away whatever unpleasantries life may bring. But, on the contrary, Porter's Pollyanna knew the secret source of strength to face adversity: by focusing on joy, as Scripture commands us to, rather than on the negatives. Timely was her message, too, since the five short years following the book's publication would bring with them the twin tragedies of world war and pandemic.

If you have been following this Isaiah 61 series, you will remember from the last two devotionals how our Lord's task force of Blessed Mourners are heirs together with Jesus Christ, the Firstborn. They possess **in Him**—according to verse 7—both great honor, and the rights and privileges of sonship, equipping them to carry forth His great commission of turning the world upside down. A heady job description, sure; but the verse doesn't end there. The "inheritance stool" does not stand on just two legs.

There's one more thing—a thing of utmost importance—that we must seize as our rightful inheritance: **everlasting joy**! Until we grasp the magnitude of the importance of the **joy** of the Lord, and allow it to flow freely from the wellspring of our heart, we will never be that City on a Hill, bringing light to the valleys of sin that surround.

If we study the major revivals of the past, we find that they evoked from the heart of man two responses: great repentance, and great joy. As a child brought up in the U.S. South during the tail end of the "Latter Rain Movement," I recall the great tent-and-sawdust revival meetings, where worshipers would pack in around the front, before the platform, singing, whooping, and dancing with the joy of the Lord. Then came the "Jesus Movement" in the late '60s and early '70s, where, once again, repentance and great joy were on full display. Topping the list of "Jesus People" worship songs were "Break Forth into Joy, O My Soul!" and "The Joy of the Lord Is My Strength."

Though space would not allow us to include the 800-plus

Scriptures about joy that Pollyanna alluded to, still, we can meditate on a choice few.

- Think about the nine Fruits of the Spirit (Galatians 5:22)—the visible evidence by which the world may see His work in our heart and come to believe in Him. The first (and greatest, as He reminds us) is **love**. But the very next, perhaps we may call it the "second greatest," is **joy**!

- During the revival of Nehemiah's time, when the people responded with open, weeping hearts to the Word of the Lord, what did he instruct them to do? "Go and celebrate with a feast of rich foods and sweet drinks, and share gifts of food with people who have nothing prepared. This is a sacred day before our Lord. Don't be dejected and sad, for the joy of the Lord is your strength!" (Nehemiah 8:10)

- How about Jesus? After all, we're studying Isaiah 61—the playbook for the earthly ministry He initiated, which He handed off to us, to be continued until His return. Well, to kick off His ministry ... He went to a party! That's right, along with His disciples and His mother, he attended a wedding, which, in those days would include a blow-out celebration with plenty of good foods, drinks, and enjoyment. And when it became clear that the caterers' error had left them short of beverages, which would certainly put a dent in the day's joy, Jesus supplied an abundance of wine—of the very best quality, as the maître d' observed!

We shall leave the theologians to debate, as they have for centuries, whether the wine they were drinking that day contained alcohol. In any case, it is irrelevant. The point is that our Lord Jesus chose—not by accident, since He has no accidents—to perform as His first miracle the act of bringing joy to the hearts of many with fine beverage for their party. And, thereby He manifested His glory so they believed in Him. (John 2:11)

And He certainly didn't stop there. We see numerous occasions in Scripture where Jesus was "eating and drinking" at this or that house. "The Son of Man has come eating and drinking, and you say, 'Look, a glutton and a winebibber, a friend of tax collectors and sinners!'" (Luke 7:34)

Of course He was no "glutton and winebibber" as His critics slanderously said of Him. Rather, He was a Person Who did not hesitate to joyfully keep company with people—of all walks of life—that He might show them the way to peace with God. This clearly stuck in the crop of the chief priests, Scribes, Pharisees, and Sadducees—who hadn't a freckle of true joy of the Lord on their whole carcass!

What's this have to do with us?

Well, consider the average Christian's daydream. Up walks his work buddy, lays a fawning hand on his shoulder and wistfully purrs, "O dear friend, you have something I don't, but I *really, really* want it!" And he has a wide-open door to lead his coworker to Jesus.

That daydream can become glorious reality right now, today, in your life and mine. But for that to happen requires that we let the Holy Spirit come in and regenerate our curmudgeonly, trash-talking, fault-finding, bellyaching selves and install that third leg of our "inheritance stool": **everlasting joy**. Then, as we truly manifest the twin fruits of love and joy ... well, **that** is when the "Nations will come to [our] light, and kings to the brightness of [our] dawn." (Isaiah 60:3)

Why not pray ...

"Dear Father,
I can no longer ignore the importance You assign to ***joy*** *in my Christian life and ministry. Please throw open the doors to my inner storehouse of negativity, and blow it all away with your divine influx of* ***everlasting joy****! That the world may see Your light in me. That the world may know Your joy.*
In Jesus' name. Amen."

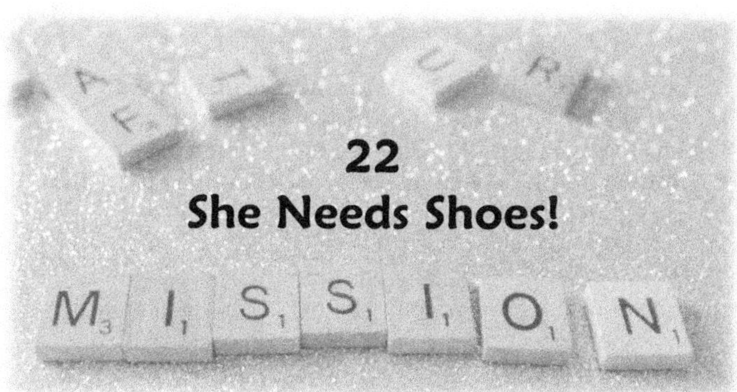

22
She Needs Shoes!

"... The LORD has anointed Me ... To console those who mourn in Zion ... For I, the Lord, love justice ..." (Isaiah 61:1b-8a)

Someone was coming. It was a girl, walking slowly and quietly, hugging the walls of shops and houses. She looked very tired, and she was carrying something. As she drew nearer, Papa Panov could see that it was a baby wrapped in a thin shawl. There was such sadness in her face and in the pinched little face of the baby, that Papa Panov's heart went out to them.

"Won't you come in," he called, stepping outside to meet them. "You both need a warm seat by the fire and a rest."

The young mother let him shepherd her indoors and to the comfort of an armchair. She gave a big sigh of relief.

He took milk from the stove and carefully fed the baby from a spoon, warming her tiny feet by the stove at the same time. "She needs shoes!" the cobbler said.

But the girl replied, "I can't afford shoes; I've got no husband to bring home money. I'm on my way to the next village to get work."

> A sudden thought flashed through Papa Panov's mind. He remembered the little shoes he had looked at last night. But he had been keeping those for Jesus. He looked again at the cold little feet and made up his mind.
>
> "Try these on her," he said, handing the baby and the shoes to the mother. The beautiful little shoes were a perfect fit.
>
> (From "Le Père Martin" ("Father Martin"), a classic folk tale by Ruben Saillens [1881], adapted by Leo Tolstoy [1885], edited by Michael Rielly [2016]; excerpted and condensed for presentation herein.)

Our expedition so far through the Isaiah 61 Messianic prophecy has covered five major themes:

- Verses 1-2: Christ's earthly ministry
- Verse 3: His recruitment of the Blessed Mourners to continue that ministry
- Verse 4: Their commission
- Verses 5-6: Their divine outfitting and provision
- Verse 7: Their firstborn inheritance in Christ

But as we arrive at verse 8, that tiny, three-letter word "**For...**" (or, "**Because...**") abruptly zooms us out to the dizzying vantage point of God's eternal perspective. "**For I, the Lord, love justice ...**" He gives us a glimpse, for the first time, of the **why** by setting the entire chapter's narrative in the context of His master plan for humanity.

How so?

Think about it: The first half of verse 8 sums up the Old Covenant: "I, the Lord, love justice; I hate robbery for burnt offering." There we have the two tenets—of "love your neighbor" and "love the Lord your God"—on which hang all the law and the prophets (Matthew 22:40).

But mankind, sold under Sin, was powerless to live up to those tenets. Which is **why** the second half of the verse pivots to the New Covenant: "I will direct their work **in truth**, and will make with them an **everlasting covenant**." It's the eternal mystery: Christ in us, the Hope of glory (Colossians 1:27), through the blood of His everlasting New Covenant, now taking residence in us and personally carrying out His Isaiah 61 commission **in truth**. No more make-believe. No more Old Covenant trial and failure.

In short, verse 8 explains **why** the Messianic Age has come. It enables us at last to attain what we never could under the Old Covenant: justice toward man and a personal relationship with God. It's the **fulfillment** of the law and the prophets.

To see what this fulfillment looks like on the New Covenant stage, we're going to unpack the four segments of verse 8 over the next few studies, starting now with the first of these four:

I, the Lord, love justice.

Now, Jesus devoted much of His teaching ministry to the importance of justice and love toward our fellow man ... arguably much more than the time He spent speaking about relationship with God. When He confronted the rich young ruler (Matthew 19), for example, He only mentioned six of the ten commandments—the ones having to do with "love your neighbor."

Why was that? Maybe our opening story can help explain!...

You may have heard this 19th-century tale before, which is also known as "The Shoemaker's Dream" or "Papa Panov's Special Christmas." It tells of a poor cobbler who, in a dream that feels incredibly real, hears Jesus promise that He will appear to him in person the next day—which is Christmas.

The shoemaker spends the day in his little shop eagerly peering out the window for Jesus' arrival. But he has many interruptions, beginning with a street sweeper stiff with cold, whom he invites inside to warm up with a cup of coffee. And, lastly—as we saw above—a destitute single mother with her hungry, half-frozen little girl who has nothing to keep her feet warm. The cobbler gives her his prize possession: a pair of child's shoes, his most excellent work, which he has treasured for many years.

As the pair leaves his shop, night is falling, and he despairs of seeing Jesus. "So, it had been just a dream after all," he thought to himself. Jesus had not come.

But the story ends with the cobbler having a waking vision of all the people who had "interrupted" his day, whom he had helped in one way or another. Followed by the voice of Jesus, same as in his dream the night before, speaking to him gently now:

"I was hungry and you fed me. I was naked and you clothed me. I was cold and you warmed me. I came to you today in every one of those you helped and welcomed."

Why not pray ...

"Dear Father,
Let me not fail to see the forest for the trees. Let me not strive to love God, Whom I cannot see, while failing to love my fellow man whom I can see. (I John 4:20) For I realize at last that we must carry one another's burdens—championing peace, love, and justice for all—and thus fulfill the law of Christ (Galatians 6:2). In the words of the old hymn: 'Oh, to be His hand extended / Reaching out to the oppressed / Let me touch Him; let me touch Jesus / So that others may know and be blessed.' Make it so, Lord God!
In Jesus' name. Amen."

23
Robbery for Burnt Offering

"... The LORD has anointed Me ... To console those who mourn in Zion ... For I, the Lord, love justice; I hate robbery for burnt offering ..." (Isaiah 61:1b-8b)

"I'm out of a job, sir, and thought maybe you might put me in the way of getting something."

"I don't know of anything. Jobs are scarce—" replied the minister, beginning to shut the door slowly.

"I didn't know but you might perhaps be able to give me a line to the city railway or the superintendent of the shops, or something," continued the young man, shifting his faded hat from one hand to the other nervously.

"It would be of no use. You will have to excuse me. I am very busy this morning. I hope you will find something. Sorry I can't give you something to do here. But I keep only a horse and a cow and do the work myself."

The Rev. Henry Maxwell closed the door and heard the man walk down the steps. As he went up into his study, he saw from his hall window that the man was going slowly down the street, still holding his hat between his hands. There was something in the figure so dejected, homeless, and forsaken that

> the minister hesitated a moment as he stood looking at it. Then he turned to his desk and with a sigh began the writing where he had left off. He had no more interruptions, and when his wife came in two hours later the sermon was finished, the loose leaves gathered up and neatly tied together, and laid on his Bible all ready for the Sunday morning service.
>
> (From *In His Steps*, [1896] Charles M. Sheldon, excerpt)

The latest stop on our Isaiah 61 Messianic tour brought us to verse 8, where Christ reveals to His Blessed Mourners the eternal why-and-wherefore of their mission to turn the world upside down. In His own words, it is because "I, the Lord, love justice; I hate robbery for burnt offering." And, having already covered, last time, the premise of **justice**—that is, to act in righteousness and love toward our fellow man—let's ponder the meaning of ...

Robbery for burnt offering!

Seriously? Like ... is our Lord's wrath revealed against those who would pilfer a goat from the neighbor's field to sacrifice at the temple?

Well, yes! ... metaphorically. See, the root of all Pharisaism—all sham piety—is our appetite for appearing "holier than thou" while having a heart of cold mutton in our dealings and relationships. As Jesus put it, "They devour widows' houses and for a show make lengthy prayers." (Luke 20:47, NIV)

We need only flip back a few pages to Isaiah chapters 58 and 59, which deal at great length with this very topic. It is, in fact, the problem statement that sets the stage for the solution laid out in Isaiah 61. It is the irredeemable faux religiosity that calls for Christ's redeeming work in the second half of verse 8 ... which we'll unpack in our next session.

So, what's a Blessed Mourner to do?

Our lead-in story above is an excerpt from the opening scene of *In His Steps*—one of the top ten best-selling Christian books of all time, after the Bible (of course) and a few others like *Pilgrim's Progress* and *Foxe's Book of Martyrs*. We're introduced to one of the main characters, Pastor Henry Maxwell, who is so intent on polishing his grandiloquent sermon that he cannot so much as spare a kind word for a homeless tramp at his door.

In His Steps. A powerhouse of truth with over 50 million copies sold, translated into more than twenty languages, and the basis for two major motion pictures. Due to a clerical error (or perhaps divine purpose), the book has been in the public domain since it was first published in 1896.

Without divulging details and spoilers—since you absolutely **must** read the book if you haven't already—suffice it to say that the drama that began with this brief conversation between a small-town pastor and a transient man ultimately snowballed into a great spiritual awakening, not only in their (fictitious) region of America, but in the heart of every man and woman over the past century who has fallen in love with this inspirational story—which compels us to antecede every word and action with the thought, "What would Jesus do?"

In effect, the resounding moral of *In His Steps* is Isaiah 61:8: "I, the Lord, love justice; I hate robbery for burnt offering."

Why not pray ...

"Dear Father,
Forgive me for all the ways I honor You with my lips while my heart is cold and distant. In every situation, in every interaction with the people you bring my way, let my prayer be, "What would the Christ of Isaiah 61 do?" And, by Your grace

and power, I commit to carrying on His eternal mission of justice and transforming love.
In Jesus' name. Amen."

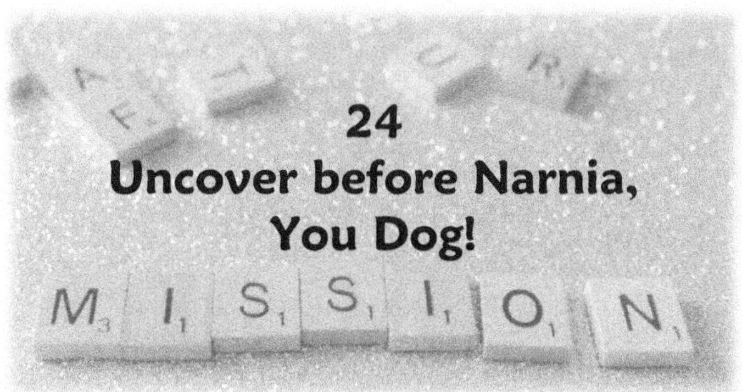

24
Uncover before Narnia, You Dog!

"... The LORD has anointed Me ... To console those who mourn in Zion ... I will direct their work in truth ..." (Isaiah 61:1b-8c)

At the castle gate Caspian [King of Narnia]'s trumpeter blew a blast and cried, "Open for the king of Narnia, come to visit his trusty and well-beloved servant, the governor of the Lone Islands...."

Only the little postern opened, and out came a tousled fellow with a dirty old hat on his head instead of a helmet, and a rusty old pike in his hand. He blinked at the flashing figures before him....

"Uncover before Narnia, you dog," thundered the Lord Bern, and dealt him a rap with his gauntleted hand which sent his hat flying from his head....

Caspian ... with Bern and Drinian and four others, went into the hall. Behind a table at the far end ... sat his Sufficiency [Gumpas], the governor of the Lone Islands.... He glanced up as the strangers entered and then looked down at his papers saying automatically, "No interviews without appointments except between nine and ten p.m. on second Saturdays."

Caspian nodded to Bern and then stood aside. Bern

and Drinian took a step forward and each seized one end of the table. They lifted it, and flung it on one side of the hall where it rolled over, scattering a cascade of letters, dossiers, ink-pots, pens, sealing-wax and documents.... Caspian at once sat down in the chair and laid his naked sword across his knees.

"My Lord," said he, fixing his eyes on Gumpas, "you have not given us quite the welcome we expected. We are the King of Narnia."

"Nothing about it in the correspondence," said the governor. "Nothing in the minutes. We have not been notified of any such thing. All irregular. Happy to consider any applications—"

"And we are come to inquire into your Sufficiency's conduct of your office," continued Caspian.... "I want to know why you have permitted this abominable and unnatural traffic in slaves to grow up here, contrary to the ancient custom and usage of our dominions...."

"Your Majesty's tender years," said Gumpas, with what was meant to be a fatherly smile, "hardly make it possible that you should understand the economic problem involved....

"Very well, then," answered Caspian, "we relieve you of your office. My Lord Bern, come here." And before Gumpas quite realised what was happening, Bern was kneeling with his hands between the King's hands and taking the oath to govern the Lone Islands in accordance with the old customs, rights, usages and laws of Narnia. And Caspian said, "I think we have had enough of governors," and made Bern a Duke, the Duke of the Lone Islands.

(From *The Voyage of the Dawn Treader*, Chapter IV [1952] C.S. Lewis, excerpt)

We have been visiting, over the past couple of episodes of our Isaiah 61 devotional series, what is indeed the hub of the entire wheel: verse 8.

Reviewing once more the structure of this verse—as articulated in devotional #22:

> Verse 8 explains **why** the Messianic Age has come. It enables us at last to attain what we never could under the Old Covenant: justice toward man and a personal relationship with God. It's the **fulfillment** of the law and the prophets.
>
> In short, the first half of verse 8, which we already studied, sums up the Old Covenant: "I, the Lord, love justice; I hate robbery for burnt offering." There we have the two tenets—of "love your neighbor" and 'love the Lord your God'—on which hang all the law and the prophets (Matthew 22:40).
>
> But mankind, sold under Sin, was powerless to live up to those tenets. Which is **why** the second half of the verse pivots to the New Covenant: "I will direct their work **in truth**, and will make with them an **everlasting covenant**." It's the eternal mystery: Christ in us, the Hope of glory (Colossians 1:27), through the blood of His everlasting New Covenant, now taking residence in us and personally carrying out His Isaiah 61 commission **in truth**. No more make-believe. No more Old Covenant trial and failure.

Today's devotional brings us to verse 8c: **"I will direct their work in truth."**

During his 64 years, the great Christian theologian C.S. Lewis wrote more than 30 books, which have sold millions of copies. But none of these holds a candle to the popularity of his seven-volume fantasy series *The Chronicles of Narnia.*

In our lead-in excerpt, which is from the third installment in that series (*The Voyage of the Dawn Treader*), the curtain opens on King Caspian of Narnia with a handful of his trusty subjects springing a surprise visit to Doorn, chief territory of the Lone Islands—a remote outpost that has belonged to the crown of Narnia for a couple of millennia.

But much like Israel under the Old Covenant, the Lone Islands had been ruled by a succession of governors such as Gumpas who, while pretending fealty to Narnia, supported human trafficking and other unjust enterprises that served to line their own pockets rather than uphold the king's law and dominion. In fact, Gumpas's allegiance was utter farce, as the story further reveals that he had never bothered to send the required tribute money to the king.

Indeed, this Narnia story mirrors the "surprise" (at least ... surprise to the chief priests, Scribes, and Pharisees) arrival of their King, recorded in Luke 4:18-21, where He declares Himself to be the long-awaited Messiah of Isaiah 61. An arrival that included cleansing the temple of make-believe worship, upsetting the money-changers' tables, disrupting their "den of robbery" (Matthew 21:13), and declaring a new era of justice and **truth** now that **He** is here!

"For I, the LORD, love justice; I hate robbery for burnt offering; **I will direct their work in truth**..." (Isaiah 61:8)

We know that these words from Isaiah are addressed specifically to His Blessed Mourners—those who stand appalled at the twin evils of injustice in the world and make-believe religiosity in the church, and who are ready to lay it all down to become agents of change.

In our story, King Caspian himself burst on the scene, ousting the disloyal Gumpas and replacing him with a trustworthy statesman, Duke Bern. Instead of a self-serving ruler, the duke would be an ambassador, a representative ... the veritable embodiment of the king.

And yet, in the real world, we know ... due to the Sin nature of Man, every well-meaning Bern has eventually morphed into a Gumpas. ***Until now!***

See, the Messiah is come, and it is **He** who will **direct our work in truth** by installing Himself, the Holy Spirit, within us.

It's "Christ in us, the Hope of glory!" (Colossians 1:27)

It's "Yet not I, but Christ liveth in me!" (Galatians 2:20)

It's what replaces "O wretched man that I am! Who will deliver me from this body of death? (Romans 7:24)" with, "...The law of the Spirit of life in Christ Jesus has made me free from the law of sin and death. For what the law could not do in that it was weak through the flesh, God did by sending His own Son in the likeness of sinful flesh, on account of sin: He condemned sin in the flesh, that the righteous requirement of the law might be fulfilled in us who do not walk according to the flesh but according to the Spirit (Romans 8:2-4, excerpts)."

THIS is why Messiah came! So Isaiah 61 could then and thenceforth be lifted from a dusty, 700-year-old prophetic scroll and fulfilled, not in make-believe, but **in truth**, "today ... in [their] hearing" (Luke 4:21)!

Why not pray ...

"Dear Father,
My prayer today, and every day, is a simple yet radical one: 'Please fill me afresh with your Holy Spirit. Burn away all empty, self-serving, make-believe piety and direct my works ***in truth****.'*
In Jesus' name. Amen."

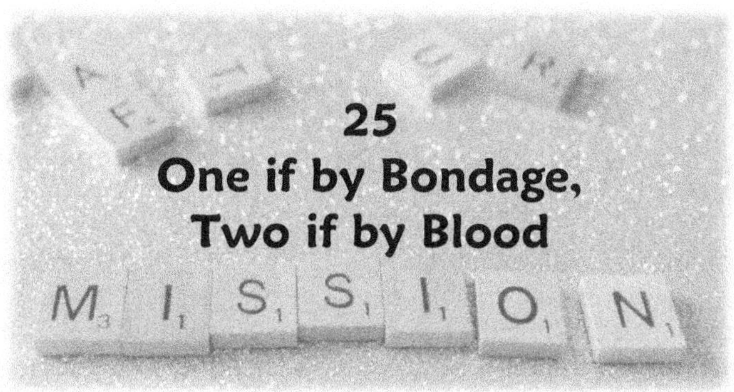

25
One if by Bondage, Two if by Blood

"... The LORD has anointed Me ... To console those who mourn in Zion ... And [I] will make with them an everlasting covenant." (Isaiah 61:1b-8d)

> **"Paul Revere, Jr. Spoon Sets World Record in $2.4 Million Fine Silver Auction!"** screamed the headline for a May 28, 2021 press release. Which continued with this opening paragraph:
>
> "Adrenaline remained high throughout Heritage Auctions' eight-hour 'Fine Silver & Objects of Vertu' Auction May 20, as one great collection followed the last. The room was electrified from the onset of the sale as an auction record was set for a single American silver spoon by America's most famous silversmith, Paul Revere, Jr. ... with the auction flying past its high estimate to reach $2,433,894."

Impressive! But what do we really know about Paul Revere?

Most of us envision this hero of the Revolution, immortalized in Henry Wadsworth Longfellow's ballad "Paul Revere's Ride," galloping through New England towns at midnight shouting his cry of alarm—something like: "The British are coming! The British are coming!"

Actually, he didn't shout at all. Though his mission was indeed to alert the townspeople, the ride itself was intentionally silent, since the countryside was crawling with Redcoats.

But Paul Revere was undeniably larger than life. Perhaps even prophetic, like the "Men of Issachar" mentioned in 1 Chronicles 12:32, who "understood the times and knew what Israel should do." Born on New Year's Day 1735, Revere took an active role at age 40 in the birth of a new nation—joining the Sons of Liberty, participating in the Boston Tea Party and, of course, undertaking his famous Midnight Ride.

On the other hand, those of us who are Antiques Roadshow junkies will be more familiar with his extraordinary Colonial-period silver work such as the spoon mentioned above—fine articles that are still with us today, consistently netting six and seven figures at black-tie auction houses.

What we may not know is that Paul Revere largely abandoned his silversmithing after the war in order to do ... so much more! He established an iron and brass foundry which supplied, among other things, material for building the U.S.S. Constitution ("Old Ironsides"). He opened a hugely successful copper rolling mill. (Think ... Revere Ware!)

OK, but what does this all have to do with our Isaiah 61 devotional series?

We have previously been examining the quadrilateral verse 8 from all facets, starting with the first three:

1. For I, the Lord, love justice;
2. I hate robbery for burnt offering;
3. I will direct their work in truth....

We've had a glimpse at the infinite depths of our Father's love, Who hates sin and injustice, and Who summons his

Blessed Mourners—deep calling to deep—to carry on His Isaiah 61 commission in **spirit and truth**. But for this divine plan to become reality requires a **new contract** with mankind. Which brings us to the fourth and final facet:

"And [I] will make with them an everlasting covenant."

Back to Paul Revere for a moment. Notice that headline, which begins with "Paul Revere, Jr."

Paul Revere, Jr.—"our" Paul Revere—was born in 1735 to a Frenchman, Apollos Rivoire, who changed his name to Paul Revere upon immigrating to America. Paul Revere Sr.—himself a fine goldsmith and silversmith—proceeded to indenture his son at the age of 13 as an apprentice in his own Boston shop. Then, in 1754, as the young man was almost finished his apprenticeship, the father passed away, which suddenly elevated Paul Revere, Jr. to the position of de facto head of the family and legal owner of the family silversmith business.

The change was subtle, and yet profound. Think about it. As a 13-year-old, and even (toward the end) a 19-year-old apprentice in his father's business, Paul Jr. was quite likely an exceptional craftsman, but a wage-earning employee nonetheless. His apprenticeship contract (indenture) gave him no right to make business decisions; it instilled in him no feeling of partnership, vision, or passion for the business.

But with the father's passing, all of that changed. There would have been a will and testament that superseded, and rendered obsolete, the apprenticeship indenture, and which now established Paul Revere, Jr. as the new owner, the **heir**. Now he could **do things**. Now he would **want to do things**.

Before, though he was a son, the working relationship was one of **bondage**: employer and employee. Now it was one of

blood: family, responsibility, and **love**. He went on to accomplish even greater things than making fine silver spoons and tea sets; he started some of the greatest American metallurgical enterprises. Why? Because now his **heart** was in it!

"Now I say that the heir, as long as he is a child, does not differ at all from a slave, though he is master of all, but is under guardians and stewards until the time appointed by the father. Even so we, when we were children, were in bondage under the elements of the world. But when the fullness of the time had come, God sent forth His Son, born of a woman, born under the law, to redeem those who were under the law, that we might receive the adoption as sons. And because you are sons, God has sent forth the Spirit of His Son into your hearts, crying out, "Abba, Father!" Therefore you are no longer a slave but a son, and if a son, then an heir of God through Christ." (Galatians 4:1-7)

That says it all, hallelujah!

But to further impress on our hearts the glorious truth of His **everlasting covenant**, which is so transcendently superior to the Old Covenant that it renders it obsolete, our Lord further articulates it for us in the book of Hebrews:

"For if that first covenant had been faultless, then no place would have been sought for a second. Because finding fault with them, He says: 'Behold, the days are coming, says the Lord, when I will make a new covenant with the house of Israel and with the house of Judah—not according to the covenant that I made with their fathers in the day when I took them by the hand to lead them out of the land of Egypt; because they did not continue in My covenant, and I disregarded them, says the Lord.

"For this is the covenant that I will make with the house of Israel after those days, says the Lord: I will put My laws in

their mind and write them on their hearts; and I will be their God, and they shall be My people. None of them shall teach his neighbor, and none his brother, saying, "Know the Lord," for all shall know Me, from the least of them to the greatest of them. For I will be merciful to their unrighteousness, and their sins and their lawless deeds I will remember no more.' In that He says, 'A new covenant,' He has made the first obsolete. Now what is becoming obsolete and growing old is ready to vanish away."
(Hebrews 8:7-13)

Why not pray ...

"Dear Father,
THANK You for calling and ordaining me to join Your Isaiah 61 corps of Blessed Mourners. Help me comprehend the length and width and height and depth of Your new and ***everlasting covenant****. Write Your law upon my heart and baptize me afresh daily in Your Holy Spirit until I live, breathe, and radiate Your love to everyone You send my way.*
In Jesus' name. Amen."

26
Seeds That Bless, Seeds That Crush

"... The LORD has anointed Me ... To console those who mourn in Zion ... And their seed shall be known among the nations, and their offspring among the peoples; all that see them shall acknowledge them, that they are the seed which Jehovah hath blessed." (Isaiah 61:1b-9)

From the ashes a fire shall be woken,
A light from the shadows shall spring;
Renewed shall be blade that was broken,
The crownless again shall be king.

(From *The Fellowship of the Ring* [1954] J.R.R. Tolkien)

When did **you** first hear the name "Tolkien"?

At the risk of dating myself, I'll confess that I discovered and devoured *The Hobbit*, followed immediately by *The Lord of the Rings* trilogy, toward the tail-end of the mid-1960s Tolkien "cult following" era. (Remember the days of "Gandalf for President!" and "Frodo Lives!" graffiti?) In fact, the set of books I read as a teen was passed to me by a former burnt-out-on-speed hippie, thankfully saved and rehabilitated during these early Jesus People years.

But it wasn't until a quarter-century later that the author came to be widely recognized—gradually and posthumously—as the "father of high fantasy literature." Fast-forward to the twenty-first century, and it would be hard to find anyone who hasn't heard of J.R.R. Tolkien, thanks in part to the magnificent Peter Jackson live-action *Lord of the Rings* film series released 2001-2003.

There were a good number of main characters in Tolkien's masterpiece saga, such as Gandalf the wizard, Frodo the hobbit, and Gollum the stoor. But the principal human character, in fact the one person this epic series revolves around in fulfilling its hidden agenda of being a Bible allegory, is Aragorn, who is the secret descendant and heir—more than 30 generations removed—of Elendil, high king of the twin realms of Gondor and Arnor.

In the next few paragraphs, we're going to see a connection between Aragorn, Adam, Abraham, Jesus Christ our Lord, and His corps of Blessed Mourners. And it all comes down to the concept of *seed.*

As we began to study verse 8 of our Isaiah 61 devotional series, we came to realize that we suddenly had a backstage pass to God's eternal perspective on the Fall of Man, Redemption, and world evangelism! And He concludes this glorious tour in verse 9 with the statement: "And their seed shall be known among the nations, and their offspring among the peoples; all that see them shall acknowledge them, that they are the seed which Jehovah hath blessed."

So, let's begin at the beginning—the Fall of Man in Genesis 3. After Adam and Eve had eaten of the forbidden tree, God showed them His eternal plan to undo the curse they had just brought upon themselves and all of mankind, and to bring back His blessing instead. He said to the serpent, "And I will put enmity between you and the woman, and between your seed and her Seed. He will crush your head, and you will strike His heel." (Genesis 3:15)

Beginning at that statement, we can trace the golden thread of redemption throughout the 66 volumes of the Bible, to where it ends with Jesus Christ's return wearing a golden crown (Revelation 14:14), as Lord of Lords and King of Kings for all eternity. And how do we recognize that thread? Again—it's all about *seed.*

When Jesus began His ministry by taking the podium in a small synagogue in Nazareth (Luke 4:18) and quoting the opening thoughts of Isaiah 61, "The Spirit of the Lord is upon Me, because He has anointed Me ..." He was throwing down the gauntlet in a dual challenge. Sure, he was flashing His credentials as the Messiah—the Anointed One—to the great annoyance of the Jewish leaders present on that day. But, more importantly, He was announcing Himself to that foul serpent, Satan, as the Seed of the woman, come to crush his head and redeem the human race for Himself.

Back to Aragorn for a moment. His credential as true heir to the joint throne of Gondor and Arnor consisted of King Elendil's broken sword, which had been passed down through thirty-plus generations of Elendil's descendants living in relative obscurity in the northern wilderness, patiently waiting for the day of restoration. That day had come, Aragorn knew, and it was time to re-forge Elendil' sword and wield it in battle to overthrow their great enemy, Sauron of Mordor, at last.

In Tolkien's words:

"The Sword of Elendil was forged anew by Elvish smiths, and on its blade was traced a device of seven stars set between the crescent Moon and rayed Sun, and about them was written many runes; for Aragorn son of Arathorn was going to war upon the marches of Mordor. Very bright was that sword when it was made whole again...."

All Aragorn had to do was reveal that shining sword to Sauron, and the war was on. And reveal it he did! (What happened next? Watch the movies or ... better yet ... read the books.) After centuries ... millennia of lying low, the rightful heir to the kingdom was coming to reclaim his own.
"But when the fullness of the time had come, God sent forth His Son, born of a woman ..." (Galatians 4:4)

So, what brings up all this talk of seed and offspring, of nations and peoples and blessing in verse 9 of Isaiah 61? Let's trace that golden thread ... because where it ends is a surprise indeed!

- As we already saw, it began in Genesis 3:15, speaking of the woman's Seed, Who would crush the serpent's head—meaning that Seed would bless all of mankind by freeing them from the bondage of Sin.

- Fast-forward to Abraham, who was the recipient of God's epic promise: "In your Seed all the nations of the earth shall be blessed, because you have obeyed My voice." (Genesis 22:18)

- Continuing through Isaac: "... And in your Seed all the nations of the earth shall be blessed." (Genesis 26:4)

- And Jacob: "... And in you and in your Seed all the families of the earth shall be blessed." (Genesis 28:14)

We're certainly seeing a pattern here. But there's more to the promise! This Seed is to be a King Whose kingdom is never-ending.

- As God first hinted to Abraham: "... And I will make nations of you, and kings shall come from you." (Genesis 17:6)

- And to Abraham's direct descendant David: "And your house and your kingdom shall be established forever before you. Your throne shall be established forever." (2 Samuel 7:16)

- And to David's direct descendant Mary: "And behold, you will conceive in your womb and bring forth a Son, and shall call His name Jesus. He will be great, and will be called the Son of the Highest; and the Lord God will give Him the throne of His father David. And He will reign over the house of Jacob forever, and of His kingdom there will be no end." (Luke 1:31-33)

- Interestingly enough, the connection was not lost on Mary: "He has helped His servant Israel, in remembrance of His mercy, as He spoke to our fathers, to Abraham and to his Seed forever." (From Mary's Song, Luke 1:54-55)

And here is where the golden thread runs right through our front door and into the hearth. Again, it has to do with the *seed.*

First, the Apostle Paul, through the Holy Spirit penned these words in Galatians 3:16: "Now to Abraham and his Seed were the promises made. He does not say, 'And to seeds,' as of many, but as of one, 'And to your Seed'—Who is Christ."

OK, so it's clear that the Seed through Whom all the nations of the earth shall be blessed is none other than the Messiah Jesus Christ. Right? Well ... *partially* right! For, just thirteen verses later, within the same chapter, Paul appears to contradict himself: "And if you are Christ's, then **you** are

Abraham's seed, and heirs according to the promise." (Galatians 3:29)

So, why does the apostle first emphasize that the promise was to Abraham's Seed—**one** Seed, Jesus Christ—and then turn around and say the opposite: that we, the **many**, are in fact Abraham's seed?

Here is where the Amplified Bible is very helpful, as it renders that same verse, Galatians 3:29: "And if you belong to Christ [if you are **in Him**], then you are Abraham's descendants, and [spiritual] heirs according to [God's] promise."

See, this is one of those cases where the English language, rich as it may be, fails us. We have a single, ambiguous grammatical construct—that of belonging, as indicated by the apostrophe-s in the example above: "Christ's"—which could mean that something is an integral part of you, or it could also mean that you simply possess it. For example, imagine for a moment that a friend confides in you, saying, "I have a skeleton." Your first response might be one of alarm: "Why ... where did you dig it up!?" When, quite obviously, every one of us has a skeleton, right? No cause for alarm there! It's part of us. Without my skeleton, I could not live. And conversely, without me, my skeleton could not live. I am in my skeleton, and my skeleton is in me; we are parts of the same entity.

So, Paul was saying that there is only **one** Seed of the woman—Seed of Abraham—Who would crush the serpent and thereby bless all peoples of the earth ... and that is Jesus the Messiah. On the other hand, if we belong to Him—meaning we are now integral parts of the same entity, members of the body of Christ—then **we** are also the Seed. And all nations of the earth shall be blessed in **us**.

In fact, Scripture goes to great lengths to hammer home this point. A couple of examples:

- "For as the body is one and has many members, but all the members of that one body, being many, are one body, so also is Christ." (1 Corinthians 12:12)

- "Abide *[live, have your very existence]* in Me, and I *[live, have My very existence]* in you. As the branch cannot bear fruit of itself, unless it abides in the vine, neither can you, unless you abide in Me. I am the vine, you are the branches. He who abides in Me, and I in him, bears much fruit; for without Me you can do nothing." (John 15:4-5, NKJV, brackets mine)

This is the same principle we encountered a few episodes back in our Isaiah 61 series, where our Lord clearly shows us that, though we are sons and daughters of God, added to His family down through the centuries, yet we do not miss out on the supreme inheritance promised to Jesus, the Firstborn—because we are **in Him**, so we are **all** firstborn!

And what about blessing all nations and peoples of the earth by crushing the head of that great serpent, Satan? Well, of course, Jesus crushed his head through His twin victories of the cross and the resurrection. But He goes on crushing—**we** go on crushing—Satan daily. We are in Him, and therefore His crushing continues through us:

- "Through God **we** will do valiantly, and it is **He** who will trample down our enemies." (Psalms 108:13)

- "The God of peace will soon crush Satan under **your** feet...." (Romans 16:20)

Hallelujah! This great triumph of our Isaiah-61 Messiah over Sin and death continues—and we, His corps of Blessed Mourners, get to be part of the campaign—until it ends on that Day when "The kingdoms of this world have become the kingdoms of our Lord and of His Christ, and He shall reign forever and ever!" (Revelation 11:15)

Why not pray ...

"Dear Father,
Thank you that my body is the temple of Christ and of Your Holy Spirit, Who dwells in me, and I in Him—so we can live and breathe, act and minister as one. Please forgive me for the frequency with which my own sin so easily besets me and hinders Your flow of blessing to all nations and peoples—specifically, the ones you have placed in my path to touch and bless. Please cleanse me of my selfishness and make me a fruitful seed, a moving part in Your eternal plan, part of that City on the Hill, a light in the darkness spreading the hope of redemption announced in Isaiah 61. In short, make me a seed that crushes *all the works of Satan and* blesses *all the nations of the earth.*
In Jesus' name. Amen."

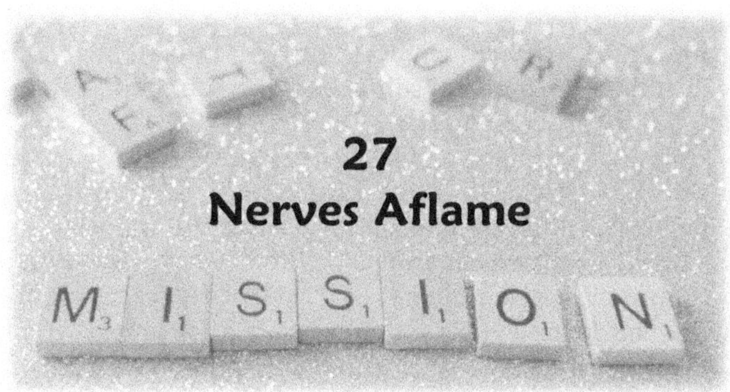

27
Nerves Aflame

"... The LORD has anointed Me ... To console those who mourn in Zion ... I will rejoice greatly in the Lord, my soul will be joyful in my God; for He has clothed me with garments of salvation, He has wrapped me with a robe of righteousness, as a groom puts on a turban, and as a bride adorns herself with her jewels." (Isaiah 61:1b-10)

> "I have one thing that counts, and which is my heart; it burns in my soul, it aches in my flesh, and it ignites my nerves: that is my love for the people and [Juan] Perón."
>
> (María Eva "Evita" Duarte de Perón [1919-1952], First Lady of Argentina)

Juan Domingo Perón ... thrice-elected, beloved and abominated ... president of Argentina. Rejecting the philosophies of both communism and capitalism (which, from his point of view, "both 'insectify' the individual by means of different systems"), he established instead the "Justicialist Party," whose principles are human dignity, freedom—for example, from corporate greed and exploitative labor conditions—and opportunity to rise out of poverty.

Whatever our opinions of Perón—regarding his questionable postulates, politics, and practices—may be, there is no

denying that he threw his heart and soul into all he did, and he was able to accomplish some amazing things.
From a *Time* Magazine article (Nov. 27, 1972):
"To his credit, Perón gave a sense of dignity to the working man for the first time in Argentine history.... Perón was able to raise wages and build hospitals, clinics and schools. He passed laws granting severance pay to discharged workers and extending social security; he also instituted the eight-hour day for farm laborers. Perón nationalized the British-owned Argentine railroads, retired the entire foreign debt, and by 1947 boasted a fivefold increase in industrial production during his regime."

Perón met his future wife, "Evita" Duarte, at a performing-arts charity event to benefit the survivors of a devastating earthquake that had claimed 10,000 lives. Evita was no stranger to injustice and heartache. Born into poverty, she was an illegitimate child (as were all her siblings), shunned and shamed by the community. Determined to rise above circumstance, she had made a successful incursion into the performing arts, which led to her participation at the charity event where she met Juan. And the rest is history!

Juan and Evita's shared passion for justice and the plight of the poor was a magnetic bond. The ensuing year would see him imprisoned by his political opponents, and then released after mass demonstrations by his supporters. The two were married on the following day and, seven months later, Evita became first lady as her husband won his first presidential election.

From that moment until her tragic death from cancer eight years later, at age 33, Evita's flaming persona captured the heart of her Argentine people. Evita Perón led rallies and gave speeches to thousands. She is credited with the passage of a bill in 1947 granting women the right to vote. And through her Eva Perón Charitable Foundation, she channeled $100 million annually to healthcare and housing for the poor.

Though she had never held elected office, Evita was given a no-holds-barred state funeral, as the nation mourned her passing ... and some even pressed to have her canonized as a saint.

So, how does any of this relate to our Isaiah 61 devotionals?

Over the past 26 segments, we have attempted to scratch the surface of this rich prophetic chapter ... though it would take many, many books to fully unpack its glorious message.

The two opening verses speak directly of Christ Jesus' arrival on the world stage. Then verse 2 quickly pivots the focus to what we have referred to as his body of Blessed Mourners—those who are deeply appalled by the state of their world and have a passion for change. Over the next seven verses, our Lord describes every detail, every facet, of the plan He has for these Mourners to turn the world upside down through the power of His Spirit.

And we now reach the part where the prophecy wraps up. First, verse 10 summarizes the Mourners' **joyful response** to their Messiah's **Covenant of Love** and His Great Commission. And finally, verse 11 recapitulates **His commitment** to them until the end of the age.

For today's segment, we will focus on one of the two points He is making in verse 10: the **Covenant of Love**. As the verse states, "... He has clothed me with garments of salvation, He has wrapped me with a robe of righteousness ..."

Think about Evita Perón and her tragic backstory. And yet, rather than letting it define her, she harnessed the wounded, mournful state of her heart to compel action for the betterment of the poor and the outcast. As she stated in our opening quote, "I have one thing that counts, and which is my heart; it burns in my soul, it aches in my flesh, and it ignites my nerves: that is my love for the people and [Juan] Perón."

Why Juan Perón? Firstly, because he shared the same love for his people. But also, because he saw Evita when she was "unseeable," when she was a lily trampled in the mud, and he cared enough to make her part of his world so they could change it together.

As Isaiah 61:10 reminds us, our Lord has clothed us with the garments of salvation (establishing His covenant with us) and wrapped us with a robe of righteousness (placing us in right standing with God, Who sees us as righteous **in Christ**).

Ponder these loving words to His people, Israel, in Ezekiel 16:

"I came by again and saw you, saw that you were ready for love and a lover. I took care of you, dressed you and protected you. I promised you my love and entered the covenant of marriage with you. I, God, the Master, gave my word. You became mine. I gave you a good bath, washing off all that old blood, and anointed you with aromatic oils. I dressed you in a colorful gown and put leather sandals on your feet. I gave you linen blouses and a fashionable wardrobe of expensive clothing. I adorned you with jewelry: I placed bracelets on your wrists, fitted you out with a necklace, emerald rings, sapphire earrings, and a diamond tiara. You were provided with everything precious and beautiful: with exquisite clothes and elegant food, garnished with honey and oil. You were absolutely stunning. You were a queen! You became world-famous, a legendary beauty brought to perfection by my adornments. Decree of God, the Master." (Ezekiel 16:8-14, MSG)

Why not pray ...

"Dear Father,
Thank You, thank You *for clothing me with salvation when I was naked in my sin, and for wrapping me in Your own*

*righteousness, precious and beautiful. Hallelujah! May Your indescribable gift of love infuse me with vision, impel me to action—**nerves aflame**—for the accomplishment of Your Great Commission, the proclamation of Your message of life in abundance, light in the darkness, and the ushering in of Your eternal kingdom.*
In Jesus' name. Amen."

28
Queen of Diamonds, King of Hearts

"... The LORD has anointed Me ... To console those who mourn in Zion ... I will greatly rejoice in the Lord, my soul shall be joyful in my God ... as a bridegroom decks himself with ornaments, and as a bride adorns herself with her jewels." (Isaiah 61:1b-10c)

"Oh, then, some pledge of your indulgence, some object which came from you and may remind me that I have not been dreaming; something you have worn, and that I may wear in my turn—a ring, a necklace, a chain."

"Will you depart if I give you that you demand ... you will leave France ... return to England?"

"I will, I swear to you."

"Wait, then, wait."

Anne of Austria re-entered her apartment, and came out again almost immediately, holding a rosewood casket in her hand, with her cipher encrusted with gold.

"Here, my Lord, here," said she, "keep this in memory of me."

Buckingham took the casket ... and faithful to the

> promise he had made, he rushed out of the apartment.
>
> (From *The Three Musketeers* [1844] Alexandre Dumas, Père)

Counted among the greatest novels ever written, *The Three Musketeers* is a fast-paced thriller brimming with romance, betrayal, palace intrigue, and derring-do.

In this pivotal scene, which occurs in the belly of the Louvre fortress, residence of Louis XIII and Queen Anne of Austria, she entertains, reluctantly at first, the advances of the Duke of Buckingham. But at last, casting caution to the winds, she slips him a tiny box that contains a fabulous ribbon brooch with twelve diamond studs—a token of love gifted to her by her husband, Louis.

It was this small act of unfaithfulness, according to Dumas's story, that catalyzed events ultimately costing reputations and lives ... even precipitating the siege of La Rochelle that began the Anglo-French war.

Today's segment of the Isaiah 61 prophecy focuses on the jubilant response of Messiah's followers—the Blessed Mourners we've been studying—to the central truth of verse 10 that we covered last time: being clothed in His salvation and wrapped in His righteousness.

And, although we've seen these faithful ones, earlier in the chapter, being endowed with joy: first, in exchange for their mourning, and again as part of their "firstborn inheritance" ... this time it's different. This is the Habakkuk-3 type of love-joy—the kind that wells up from within and bursts forth in response to **who** we are in the Beloved, regardless of our station or circumstance:

> Though the fig tree does not bud
>   and there are no grapes on the vines,
> Though the olive crop fails
>   and the fields produce no food,
> Though there are no sheep in the pen
>   and no cattle in the stalls,
> **Yet I will rejoice in the Lord,**
>   **I will be joyful in God my Savior.**
> The Sovereign Lord is my strength;
> He makes my feet like the feet of a deer,
> He enables me to tread on the heights.
> (Habakkuk 3:17-19, NIV)

In fact, the prophet Habakkuk's words (7th century B.C.) match those of Isaiah 61 (8th century B.C.): "**I will greatly rejoice in the Lord, my soul shall be joyful in my God** ... as a bridegroom decks himself with ornaments, and as a bride adorns herself with her jewels."

So, the metaphor is that we flaunt this boundless love-joy—which is to be found **in** Christ—just as a bride adorns herself with the glittering jewelry she has received from the bridegroom on her wedding day. She's head-over-heels in love, and the world must know and rejoice with her!

But then comes the sad and fateful scene ... where we find the exquisite royal bride, Anne of Austria, trysting in a dark passageway with the enemy of her homeland—the enemy of her husband and lover, King Louis—and handing over the priceless diamond jewelry he'd gifted to her. The same jewelry she had worn with delight just twelve years ago.

Anne of Austria's romantic feelings for her husband didn't evaporate in a day, or even a year. But when she failed to guard her heart, it was simply a matter of time—a "slow fade."

"It's a slow fade when you give yourself away.
It's a slow fade when black and white have turned to gray
And thoughts invade, choices made,

A price will be paid when you give yourself away.
People never crumble in a day."
(From "Slow Fade" [2007] Casting Crowns)

Let us ponder the heartbroken words of our Lord in Revelation 2: "And you have persevered and have patience, and have labored for My name's sake and have not become weary. Nevertheless, I have this against you, that you have left your first love. Remember therefore from where you have fallen; repent and do the first works...."

Why not pray ...

"Dear Father,
Thinking back to my first love, when my heart brimmed with joy like a bride in shining jewelry ... I can only echo the words of the songwriter:
'Help me, Jesus; I know what I am. / Now that I know that I've needed You so / Help me, Jesus, my soul's in Your hand.'
I repent of my unfaithful neglect. In Your tender mercy, take me by the hand and lead me back. May I know that first love, do those first works, and rejoice once again in God my Savior, King of Hearts!
In Jesus' name. Amen."

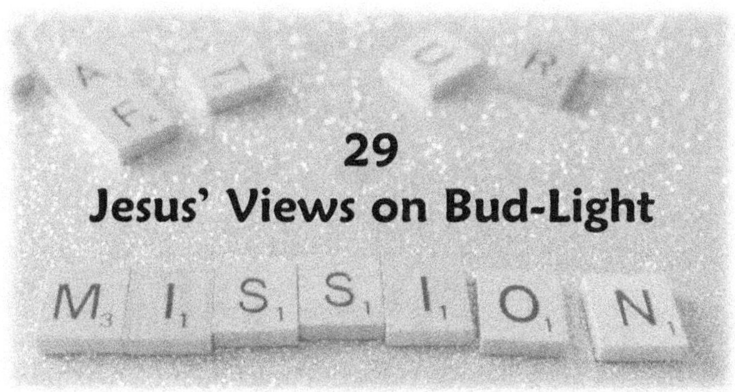

29
Jesus' Views on Bud-Light

"... The LORD has anointed Me ... To console those who mourn in Zion ... For as the earth brings forth its bud, as the garden causes the things that are sown in it to spring forth, so the Lord God will cause righteousness and praise to spring forth before all the nations." (Isaiah 61:1b-11)

> Then, without warning, [the witch] did a thing that was dreadful to see.... She stretched up her right arm and wrenched off one of the cross-bars of the lamp-post.
>
> . . .
>
> She raised her arm and flung the iron bar straight at its head.... The bar struck the Lion fair between the eyes. It glanced off and fell with a thud in the grass.
>
> . . .
>
> "Hullo! What's that?" said Digory.... "Do come and look...."
>
> It was a perfect little model of a lamp-post, about three feet high but lengthening, and thickening in proportion, as they watched it; in fact growing just as the trees had grown.
>
> "It's alive too—I mean, it's lit," said Digory.
>
> "Remarkable, most remarkable," muttered Uncle Andrew.... "We're in a world where everything,

> even a lamp-post, comes to life and grows...."
> "Don't you see?" said Digory. "This is where the bar fell—the bar she tore off the lamp-post at home...."
>
> (From *The Magician's Nephew*, Chapters VIII and IX [1955] C.S. Lewis, excerpts)

As our tour of the Isaiah 61 Messianic prophecy comes in for a landing, He closes it with one final thought. This thought addresses the question that the ten preceding verses have ignited in the minds of His Blessed Mourners: "How could I dream of fulfilling even a molecule of this weighty mandate? Surely I'll fall flat."

Have no fear. Is this not the same dear Savior Who said, "Take My yoke upon you and learn from Me, for I am gentle and lowly in heart, and you will find rest for your souls. For My yoke is easy and My burden is light"? (Matthew 11:29-30) Even as He calls us to submit our neck to His toilsome yoke, He assures us that the labor will be restful, easy, and light! But how can this be?

Let's unpack our Lord's concluding message in verse 11, which settles this very mystery: "For as the earth brings forth its bud, as the garden causes the things that are sown in it to spring forth, so the Lord God will cause righteousness and praise to spring forth before all the nations."

First, think of a **bud**, on a **branch**, connected to a **vine** in the earth of the Lord's garden. "I am the vine; you are the branches. Whoever abides in Me and I in him, he it is that bears much fruit, for apart from Me you can do nothing." (John 15:5, ESV) See, as branches we often flaunt lots of **buds**, which are our good intentions—all the things we're going to accomplish "for Jesus." But those buds will never develop into a single piece of fruit without the power of the **vine** coursing through us.

This is a sobering thought, and yet ... what freedom, what exuberance, what "joy unspeakable" it unleashes in us when we finally "**get it**"! It's our Lord Who is at work in us, both to **will** (the bud, the good intention) and to **fulfill** (the cluster bursting forth in sweet fruit) His good pleasure. We need only be planted in His good earth, where the "the garden" itself—the very earth, charged with His infinite love and power—"causes the things that are sown in it to spring forth."

Theologian and author C.S. Lewis, best known for his classic fiction series *The Chronicles of Narnia*, gave us a unique illustration of this truth. If you've read the first installment of the Narnia books (*The Lion, the Witch, and the Wardrobe*) or seen one of the video adaptations, you will recall Lucy's discovery, when she first enters Narnia, of a lamp-post strangely located and shining bright in the middle of a forest.

Though that book was the first of the Narnia series to be published, it was followed five years later by a prequel (the sixth book of the series, *The Magician's Nephew*), where we discover at last the origin of this odd lamp-post.

In true allegorical style, the story brings us to the land of Narnia at the dawn of its creation, in a state of utter darkness and void. And there we find Aslan the Lion (a type of Jesus) speaking—or singing, as it were—all things into being. His words permeate the earth itself, which responds in explosive fashion with every sort of grass, trees, flowers, and herbs.

Enter the witch Jadis (the story's counterpart for Satan) appearing on the scene from another dimension. In a burst of hatred and wrath at finding Aslan and hearing His creation song, she flings at Him the only thing that comes to hand—a short iron bar that had earlier been wrenched from a lamp-post. It ricochets off the Lion's head, Who is both unharmed and unruffled by the blow. But almost immediately, as the iron sticks into the earth pregnant with Aslan's creation power, it begins growing into a fully-formed lamp-post that sheds a magnificent, sweet **light** in the manner of its kind.

Isaiah 61 is all about Messiah Jesus, Who said, "I am the Light of the World" (John 8:12), coming to dispel darkness and despair. But He also said, "As the Father sent **Me**, so I send **you**" (John 20:21), and "**You** are the light of the world" (Matthew 5:14). We not only carry His torch ... we **are** the torch as His Spirit shines bright in us. We not only purvey His fruit of hope and salvation ... we **are** the branches, that bear the buds, that spring forth into the most delicious fruits of "righteousness and praise ... before all the nations." How? Solely by virtue of abiding in Him—in His earth, in His garden—where His Isaiah 61 creation power courses through our veins.

In the words of the old hymn: *"Channels only, blessed Master / But with all Thy wondrous power / Flowing through us, Thou canst use us / Every day and every hour."*

Why not pray ...

"Dear Father,
What a fitting conclusion You sealed the Isaiah 61 message with, hallelujah! Help me to "get it." I need to "get it"! Open the eyes of my heart to see that I, too—flawed and failure-prone as I am—can be a branch budding forth to glorious fruit, a light springing up in the darkness, as I yield to Your loving hand, to be rooted in the fertile earth of Your garden. In Jesus' name. Amen."

30
Megatonnage!

"... The LORD has anointed Me ... To console those who mourn in Zion ... And they shall rebuild ... raise up ... and repair ..." (Isaiah 61:1b-4)

If you could add together the power of prayer of the people just in this room, what would be its megatonnage?...

This power of prayer can be illustrated by a story that goes back to the fourth century. The Asian monk [Telemachus] living in a little remote village, spending most of his time in prayer or tending the garden from which he obtained his sustenance.... And then one day, he thought he heard the voice of God telling him to go to Rome. And believing that he had heard, he set out. And weeks and weeks later, he arrived there, having traveled most of the way on foot.

And it was at a time of a festival in Rome. They were celebrating a triumph over the Goths. And he followed a crowd into the Colosseum, and then there in the midst of this great crowd, he saw the gladiators come forth, stand before the Emperor, and say, "We who are about to die salute you." And he realized they were going to fight to the death for the entertainment of the crowds. And he cried out, "In the name of Christ, stop!" And his voice was lost in the tumult there in the great Colosseum.

> And as the games began, he made his way down through the crowd and climbed over the wall and dropped to the floor of the arena. Suddenly the crowds saw this scrawny little figure making his way out to the gladiators and saying, over and over again, "In the name of Christ, stop." And they thought it was part of the entertainment, and at first they were amused. But then, when they realized it wasn't, they grew belligerent and angry. And as he was pleading with the gladiators, "In the name of Christ, stop," one of them plunged his sword into his body. And as he fell to the sand of the arena in death, his last words were, "In the name of Christ, stop."
>
> And suddenly, a strange thing happened. The gladiators stood looking at this tiny form lying in the sand. A silence fell over the Colosseum. And then, someplace up in the upper tiers, an individual made his way to an exit and left, and others began to follow. And in the dead silence, everyone left the Colosseum. That was the last battle to the death between gladiators in the Roman Colosseum. Never again did anyone kill or did men kill each other for the entertainment of the crowd.
>
> One tiny voice that could hardly be heard above the tumult. "In the name of Christ, stop!"
>
> (Ronald Reagan, "Remarks at the Annual National Prayer Breakfast" [February 2, 1984], from ReaganLibrary.gov, excerpts)

There are varying accounts of the precise events of that day, which history suggests was January 1 of A.D. 391. Some have it that the gladiators skewered Telemachus at the command of a Roman official. Others recount that it was the crowd themselves who stoned him to death (unlikely though it may seem that they would find a supply of stones for that purpose within the Colosseum). But the end result of his actions—and of his death—is a matter of recorded fact. Touched to the heart by Telemachus's courage and martyrdom, Emperor Honorius issued the edict that banned gladiatorial combat within the empire for all time.

In this concluding installment of our study of Isaiah 61, the "Messianic Playbook," we could perhaps review the chapter's main elements, ponder our Lord's marvelous and compassionate plan of redemption, or reiterate our duty to spread His message as long as we have breath left in us to do so. But more to the point, let's take this opportunity to address a more practical angle: "What is the likelihood that, thirty days from now, I will even remember what I've learned from Isaiah 61 ... much less be putting it into practice?"

"Anyone who listens to the Word but does not do what it says is like someone who looks at his face in a mirror and, after looking at himself, goes away and immediately forgets what he looks like." (James 1:23-24, NIV)

Uh-oh!

But **why** is it that we so often listen to the Word being taught, or preached on a Sunday morning, and then have absolutely no recollection thirty days later of what our Lord was saying to us through that teaching or sermon? Why is it that we can read a profound Christian book, or even a chapter of the Bible, and hear His voice almost audibly saying, *"This is your life purpose. Listen up! Repent and seek God! Obey!"* ... and never take the slightest action in response to that call?

Our Savior's patience is never-ending (hallelujah!), and He is not One to condemn, but to train, encourage, and draw us to Himself as a loving Father. And, as we survey the magnitude of the human Problem—for which He has called us to be part of the solution—He knows that we are "but flesh," that we naturally grow faint and discouraged at our own inadequacy.

And yet, Christian, if you have felt Him tug at your heart through this Isaiah 61 study ... if there was ever a time to respond, it is now, in light of the glorious message of the chapter that describes how He intends to use His corps of Blessed Mourners to be salt and light, to turn an upside-down world right side up. This is our purpose. This is why we haven't been raptured or otherwise swept into eternity with Him. Because **this** is the work we have yet to do. And there's never a job He would call us to without also providing the courage and the power to do it! As Jesus said—His last words of commission to His disciples in Matthew 28—"And surely I am with you always, to the very end of the age."

So, what is the root cause of our paralysis when it comes to matters such as these? Surely, it's a simple one: where to start! What could I do in my lifetime that would move the needle on world peace? World hunger? World revival? What could I possibly do to stop seven thousand runaway trains in our nation today, all heading toward the precipice of disaster and divine judgment? *And that, in fact, is the right question to ask.*

Remember when the prophet Elijah, toward the end of his life, poured out his discouraged heart to God saying, "I'm the only one left who serves You?" And God's loving reply was, "There are *seven thousand* others who are faithful. You are not the only one!" ... as He sent Elijah on his way to meet up with a few of those seven thousand and partner with them for the task at hand. (1 Kings 19:14-16)

See, it's 100% true that we are incapable, alone and in ourselves, of stopping seven thousand runaway trains. But if each of us seven thousand faithful ones that God has reserved and called to be His Blessed Mourners ... if each of us sets his or her hand to a **single** track switch, and if we all act in obedience to throw that switch—be it ever so long and tedious a task—we will, in the end, succeed in redirecting those seven thousand trains off the track that leads to perdition, saving the helpless souls aboard who were deceived and doomed by the enemy's lies.

Think of Telemachus, who could not have imagined how successful he would be at throwing a switch that day, bringing the train of gladiatorial deaths to a halt. He just acted in obedience on what he felt called to do. And God did the rest.

We can think of many others who tackled a single task, whether great or small, and God did the rest: Mother Theresa, Dr. Martin Luther King, Jr., William Wilberforce, George Washington Carver, Harriet Beecher Stowe ... the list is endless. Put them all together, and the aggregate result is, to use President Ronald Reagan's words, "**megatonnage**!"

In conclusion of this devotional—and of the entire Isaiah 61 study—here is a short piece I posted in 2012 on the National Minute of Prayer website (MinuteofPrayer.org):

GOD'S HEART IS TOO BIG

Since the *The Big Ben Minute* [book] was released this spring, a number of media folks have asked me about the Minute of Prayer movement. What's the bottom line ... what's the angle? Is this about praying to end abortion? Our loss of freedoms? The upcoming election? The war on terror?

The answer is YES. And a thousand, thousand other things we Christians should be caring about and fervently praying for.

But, how do we cover all that ground in 60 seconds? Why, it would be absurd to think we could effectively do such a thing. Think about it....

Just as our Father God keeps countless worlds in motion, while His eye is on the fallen sparrow, likewise, His heart swells with compassion for each of the seven billion humans on this planet—including the three hundred million of us who live in the United States of America.

- Each time a young person is cut down in the prime of life by a bullet or a bomb on the battlefield, He is right there, feeling the pain that mankind's sin has brought on our world.

- Each time a tender baby is savagely poisoned or torn limb from limb by an abortion procedure, God is there feeling the agony and bearing the infant away in His everlasting arms.

- Each time a young lady sits alone, cutting her body with razors to express the pang of loneliness in her soul, or a young man pumps destructive chemicals into his veins in an attempt to soothe the misery of his existence for just an hour ...

- When the hopeless newborn gasps for air in a dumpster ...

- Or the carefree girl is dragged into an alley at gunpoint ...

- Or the young couple loads that last cardboard box into the car and drives away from their home in despair, because the bank has taken possession ...

- Or the doctor calls, and yes, it's malignant ...

Our Father God's heart weeps for the pain of all who are oppressed by the devil, and He desires to saturate us with His compassion so we may intercede for their release. But His heart is too big. If He were to saddle any one of us, even for a moment, with the sorrow He feels for lost humanity, it would crush us!

What, then? There's an old hymn that opens with

the words: *"Lord, lay some soul upon my heart / And love that soul through me."*

You see, God will take one splinter of that massive cross of mankind's suffering, and He'll lay it on you or me. And, we always know what splinter He's placed in our heart, because it pinches deeply each time we think about it! Your splinter might be the vacuum of godly leadership in our nation. Mine might be the 3000+ babies cruelly slaughtered each day in the U.S. alone—or maybe it's the countless young ladies who can never seem to wash their hands of the guilt over ending a child's life. Another's splinter might be the homeless young families sheltering in the old condemned post office building down the street.

So, when my alarm buzzes at 9:00 p.m., calling me to join my voice with the invisible throng across our nation who are praying at this same moment, I hold up my splinter to the One who gave it. And, as each of us holds up his or her splinter, the cross of God's compassion takes shape in our corporate prayer. That's when Heaven and Earth touch, and the infinite heart of our loving Father connects with His people's supplication. And that's when He can start to move across America, in every broken heart, and broken home, and broken church, and broken state, to bring hope and deliverance.

What, then, is the "bottom line"? What's the purpose of our Minute of Prayer? It's to pray for whatever splinter of burden God has laid on each of us. That, ultimately, He may forgive our sin and heal our land.

Why not pray ...

"Dear Father,
As I stood these thirty days before the mirror that is Isaiah 61, I studied my own face and said, 'Could I possibly be one of the

Blessed Mourners my Lord is referring to? Could I possibly make a difference?' Now I must needs step away from that mirror. But please ... burn the image into my soul. Don't stop working on me, drawing me, changing me, refining me like silver in Your furnace every single day, until you purify and draw out a precious nugget that reflects Your image ... Your heart for the lost.
In Jesus' name. Amen."

ABOUT THE AUTHOR

Brad Fenichel is an author, freelance writer, and speaker. He is founder and president of Saddle Mountain Communications, reaching America with a message of living prayer and a passion for revival in our generation.

Brad's is the author of *Curse of the Skunk People*, and he has also republished *The Big Ben Minute*, a 1943 WWII-era classic, by special permission of the author's two sons. Both books are available on Amazon.com.

Brad's next book, *Mighty*, is due out within a year of this book's publication.

Brad is also a spokesman for the National Minute of Prayer—a grassroots effort calling Americans everywhere to 1 minute of daily prayer for revival. For information on how you can become a "Minute-Man," visit the National Minute of Prayer website at www.MinuteOfPrayer.org.

Brad lives in rural Cecil County, Maryland with his wife Janette and three dysfunctional cats.

To contact Brad, visit his blog: www.StrikeTheJordan.org.

NOTES

NOTES

NOTES

NOTES

www.ingramcontent.com/pod-product-compliance
Lightning Source LLC
LaVergne TN
LVHW051408080426
835508LV00022B/2983

9781955510028